mentoring for meaningful results

Asset-Building Tips, Tools, and Activities for Youth and Adults

KRISTIE PROBST

Search INSTITUTE | *Practical research benefiting children and youth*

Mentoring for Meaningful Results:
Asset-Building Tips, Tools, and Activities for Youth and Adults

By Kristie Probst
Copyright © 2006 by Search Institute

The following are registered trademarks of Search Institute:
Search Institute®, Developmental Assets®,
and Healthy Communities • Healthy Youth®.

10 9 8 7 6 5 4 3 2
Printed on acid-free paper in the United States of America.

Search Institute
615 First Avenue Northeast, Suite 125
Minneapolis, MN 55413
www.search-institute.org
612-376-8955 • 800-888-7828

ISBN-13: 978-1-57482-875-7
ISBN-10: 1-57482-875-4

Credits
Editor: Tenessa Gemelke
Book Design: Percolator
Production Coordinator: Mary Ellen Buscher

Library of Congress Cataloging-in-Publication Data
Probst, Kristie.
    Mentoring for meaningful results : asset-building tips, tools, and activities for youth and adults / Kristie Probst.
        p. cm.
    Includes bibliographical references and index.
    ISBN-10: 1-57482-875-4 (pbk. : alk. paper)
    ISBN-13: 978-1-57482-875-7 (pbk. : alk. paper)
    1. Social work with youth—United States. 2. Mentoring—United States. 3. Youth—Counseling of—United States. I. Title.
    HV1431.P76 2006
    362.7—dc22   2005031339

About Search Institute

Search Institute is an independent, nonprofit, nonsectarian organization whose mission is to provide leadership, knowledge, and resources to promote healthy children, youth, and communities. The institute collaborates with others to promote long-term organizational and cultural change that supports its mission. For a free information packet, call 800-888-7828.

About This Resource

The content of this resource was developed with input from individuals at Big Brothers Big Sisters of the Greater Twin Cities, Colby Cares about Kids, Maine Mentoring Partnership, Mentoring Partnership of Minnesota, Mentoring USA, MENTOR/National Mentoring Partnership, and other organizations. Search Institute is grateful for insights from these valuable partners.

Licensing and Copyright

Printing Tips

To produce high-quality copies of activity sheets for distribution without spending a lot of money, follow these tips:

• Always copy from the original. Copying from a copy lowers the reproduction quality.

• Make copies more appealing by using brightly colored paper or even colored ink. Quick-print shops often run daily specials on certain colors of ink.

• For variety, consider printing each activity sheet on a different color of paper.

• If you are using more than one activity sheet or an activity sheet that runs more than one page, make two-sided copies.

• Make sure the paper is heavy enough (use at least 60-pound offset paper) so that the words don't bleed through (e.g., as often happens with 20-pound paper).

contents

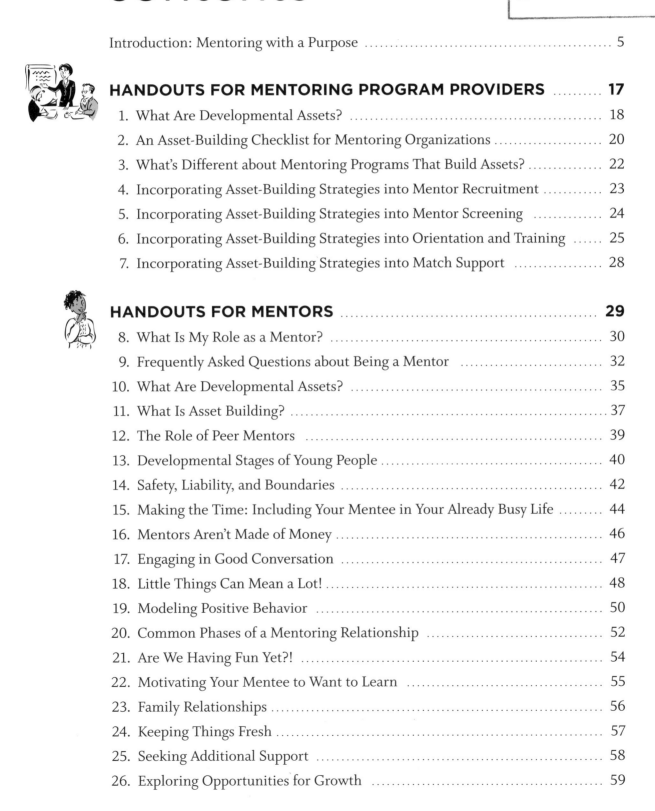

introduction

MENTORING WITH A PURPOSE

When Kay Hong applied to be a mentor at St. Joseph's Home for Children in St. Paul, Minnesota, she was like many volunteers: caring and hopeful, but uncertain about her role. She initially pictured herself reading books and giving hugs to young children; however, when she was officially invited to be a participant, the only openings they had were in a new group-mentoring program for teenage boys. Kay accepted the assignment but wondered privately what she had to offer older boys. She looked forward to the one-day training event, hoping she'd be reassured.

The training began with information about the organization and about the boys: Many were from homes troubled by mental illness, poverty, and abuse, and many were doing poorly in school and were involved in risky behaviors like drug use and drinking. Once again Kay wondered, more seriously now, how she could possibly help with all of those problems.

Then the next portion of the training introduced the new mentors to Search Institute's framework of 40 Developmental Assets™. Kay would later become an editor at Search Institute, but this was her first introduction to the concept of assets. As they read through and discussed these positive qualities, experiences, and opportunities that all young people need in their lives, the list enabled her to see that her role as a mentor was not to provide *all* of the good things kids need, but to assist in providing whichever ones she could. For example, she might help the boys find books they would like (Asset 25, Reading for Pleasure), or talk with them about the meanings of life and what they might want to do for work in the future (Asset 39, Sense of Purpose). She could finally imagine how she might fit into the life of a teenage boy.

As she looks back at the training now, Kay remembers that she was more than reassured—she was energized. She began her mentoring experience with a sense that there was much she could do to make a difference. Moving forward with renewed confidence, Kay and one mentee forged a rich relationship that lasted several years.

Mentoring for Meaningful Results: Asset-Building Tips, Tools, and Activities for Youth and Adults offers you an exploration of the power of *asset building*, the notion that every caring adult has a role in building Developmental Assets for and with young people, and young people can play a big part in building assets for themselves and others. Program leaders, mentors, mentees, and families of mentees can all benefit from a richer mentoring experience when they incorporate this positive approach. This book contains valuable tools for creating a rich and caring environment in which young people can find the things they need to learn, grow, and flourish.

DEVELOPMENTAL ASSETS: A POWERFUL TOOL FOR SHAPING HIGH-QUALITY MENTORING PROGRAMS

The Developmental Assets framework began with a simple question: What is it that young people need to grow up healthy? As Karen Pittman of The Forum for Youth Investment suggests, we can understand "healthy" to mean not only as problem-free as possible but—more important—fully prepared to be responsible and productive citizens. Search Institute's list of 40 Developmental Assets describes positive skills, experiences, and opportunities that help young people grow into caring, confident adults.

People have traditionally viewed youth-serving programs such as mentoring programs in terms of their role in preventing and curtailing the potential problems youth face. This has been particularly true for programs designed for older youth and adolescents. A growing movement among researchers and those who work with youth points to an expanded role for programs that serve youth in the out-of-school hours. While embracing prevention and safety as vital aspects of a good mentoring program, the positive youth development movement takes a more holistic view of youth and the power of youth programs to ensure access to an interrelated range of experiences, relationships, and skills all youth need to grow up healthy.

Since its founding in 1958, Search Institute has been a key agent in the positive youth development movement. Individuals, organizations, and communities seeking to implement a positive approach to raising competent and caring young people have adopted the framework of 40 Developmental Assets. Because the Developmental Assets constitute a conceptual framework, any individual, program, organization, or community can incorporate the concepts in shaping efforts to provide all youth with the essential elements of healthy development.

In exploring the question of what youth need to grow up healthy, Search Institute has done extensive research, reviewing more than 1,200 studies from major bodies of literature, including prevention, resilience, and adolescent development, to identify what young people need to thrive. Institute researchers have documented that young people who are healthy, whether they come from the poorest or the wealthiest environments and from diverse ethnic and cultural groups, have certain meaningful elements in their lives. Researchers identified eight categories that describe these elements:

- The solid presence of **support** from others;
- A feeling of **empowerment;**
- A clear understanding of **boundaries and expectations;**
- Varied opportunities for **constructive use of time;**
- A strong **commitment to learning;**
- An appreciation of **positive values;**
- Sound **social competencies;** and
- A personal sense of **positive identity.**[1,2]

Moreover, research conducted by Search Institute consistently shows that the strengths described within these categories provide a solid foundation for positive development and academic success, and that their presence helps protect youth from engaging in risky behavior and promotes acting in productive ways. The institute identified 40 different components and gave the name "Developmental Assets" to these building blocks of healthy youth development. The data consistently show that the power of assets is cumulative: The more assets young people report experiencing, the more apt they are to succeed in school and live positive lives, and the less likely they are to participate in high-risk behaviors such as drug use, violence, and early sexual activity.

When adults make deliberate efforts to help young people increase the number and degree of Developmental Assets they experience in their lives, it is called *asset building*. As mentoring programs strive to reduce risky behaviors and increase positive outcomes for youth, asset building is a powerful approach for helping youth acquire the skills and experiences they need. The Developmental Assets framework and the asset-building approach have been used by hundreds of communities, as well as numerous organizations and individuals, to identify assets they are already building and where they might make changes in their work to provide a healthier, more nurturing environment for young people. Mentoring programs can also use the framework to bring out and support the best in the young people they serve.

The assets have slightly varied definitions for different age groups, and these are shown on pages 8–11. As you read through the items that involve parents, you may recognize that many young people experience "parental" relationships with grandparents, older siblings, or other family members. Review the lists and imagine for a moment how many of the assets are or might be available to young people in your mentoring program.

THE POWER OF DEVELOPMENTAL ASSETS

In addition to identifying the Developmental Assets and organizing them into a cohesive framework, Search Institute has surveyed more than two million young people in hundreds of U.S. and Canadian communities to measure the impact of assets on their lives. Lower levels of assets correspond with risky behaviors such as violence, early sexual activity, and drug use; on the other hand, higher levels of assets are linked with successful, healthy youth. The correlation between assets and behavior holds true across all indicators in the survey regardless of a young person's gender, school size, geographic region, socioeconomic status, community size, or race/ethnicity. In other words, the more assets, the better. (See "The Power of Assets" on page 12.)

The strong connection between levels of assets and young people's behaviors and attitudes is the good news; it reinforces the importance of what many mentoring programs already do and suggests that by providing access to more assets, we can have a greater impact on the direction of young people's lives. The bad news, unfortunately, is that young people are not experiencing enough of these developmental building blocks.

40 Developmental Assets for Middle Childhood

WITH DEFINITIONS (STUDENTS IN GRADES 4-6)

EXTERNAL ASSETS

SUPPORT

1. **Family Support**—Family life provides high levels of love and support.

2. **Positive Family Communication**—Parent(s) and child communicate positively. Child feels comfortable seeking advice and counsel from parent(s).

3. **Other Adult Relationships**—Child receives support from adults other than her or his parent(s).

4. **Caring Neighborhood**—Child experiences caring neighbors.

5. **Caring School Climate**—Relationships with teachers and peers provide a caring, encouraging school environment.

6. **Parent Involvement in Schooling**—Parent(s) are actively involved in helping the child succeed in school.

EMPOWERMENT

7. **Community Values Children**—Child feels valued and appreciated by the adults in the community.

8. **Children as Resources**—Child is included in decisions at home and in the community.

9. **Service to others**—Child has opportunities to help others in the community.

10. **Safety**—Child feels safe at home, at school, and in her or his neighborhood.

BOUNDARIES AND EXPECTATIONS

11. **Family Boundaries**—Family has clear and consistent rules and consequences and monitors the child's whereabouts.

12. **School Boundaries**—School provides clear rules and consequences.

13. **Neighborhood Boundaries**—Neighbors take responsibility for monitoring the child's behavior.

14. **Adult Role Models**—Parent(s) and other adults in the child's family, as well as nonfamily adults, model positive, responsible behavior.

15. **Positive Peer Influence**—Child's closest friends model positive, responsible behavior.

16. **High Expectations**—Parent(s) and teachers expect the child to do her or his best at school and in other activities.

CONSTRUCTIVE USE OF TIME

17. **Creative Activities**—Child participates in music, art, drama, or creative writing two or more times per week.

18. **Child Programs**—Child participates two or more times per week in cocurricular activities or structured community programs for children.

19. **Religious Community**—Child attends religious programs or services one or more times per week.

20. **Time at Home**—Child spends some time most days both in high-quality interaction with parent(s) and doing things at home other than watching TV or playing video games.

CONTINUES →

40 Developmental Assets for Middle Childhood

WITH DEFINITIONS (STUDENTS IN GRADES 4-6)

INTERNAL ASSETS

COMMITMENT TO LEARNING

21. **Achievement Motivation**—Child is motivated and strives to do well in school.

22. **Learning Engagement**—Child is responsive, attentive, and actively engaged in learning at school and enjoys participating in learning activities outside of school.

23. **Homework**—Child usually hands in homework on time.

24. **Bonding to Adults at School**—Child cares about teachers and other adults at school.

25. **Reading for Pleasure**—Child enjoys and engages in reading for fun most days of the week.

POSITIVE VALUES

26. **Caring**—Parent(s) tell the child it is important to help other people.

27. **Equality and Social Justice**—Parent(s) tell the child it is important to speak up for equal rights for all people.

28. **Integrity**—Parent(s) tell the child it is important to stand up for one's beliefs.

29. **Honesty**—Parent(s) tell the child it is important to tell the truth.

30. **Responsibility**—Parent(s) tell the child it is important to accept personal responsibility for behavior.

31. **Healthy Lifestyle**—Parent(s) tell the child it is important to have good health habits and an understanding of healthy sexuality.

SOCIAL COMPETENCIES

32. **Planning and Decision Making**—Child thinks about decision making and is usually happy with the result of her or his decisions.

33. **Interpersonal Competence**—Child cares about and is affected by other people's feelings, enjoys making friends, and, when frustrated or angry, tries to calm her- or himself.

34. **Cultural Competence**—Child knows and is comfortable with people of different racial, ethnic, and cultural backgrounds and with her or his own cultural identity.

35. **Resistance Skills**—Child can stay away from people who are likely to get her or him in trouble and is able to say no to doing wrong or dangerous things.

36. **Peaceful Conflict Resolution**—Child attempts to resolve conflict nonviolently.

POSITIVE IDENTITY

37. **Personal Power**—Child feels he or she has some influence over things that happen in her or his life.

38. **Self-Esteem**—Child likes and is proud to be the person he or she is.

39. **Sense of Purpose**—Child sometimes thinks about what life means and whether there is a purpose for her or his life.

40. **Positive View of Personal Future**—Child is optimistic about her or his personal future.

40 Developmental Assets for Adolescents

WITH DEFINITIONS (STUDENTS IN GRADES 6–12)

EXTERNAL ASSETS

SUPPORT

1. **Family Support**—Family life provides high levels of love and support.

2. **Positive Family Communication**—Young person and her or his parent(s) communicate positively, and young person is willing to seek advice and counsel from parent(s).

3. **Other Adult Relationships**—Young person receives support from three or more nonparent adults.

4. **Caring Neighborhood**—Young person experiences caring neighbors.

5. **Caring School Climate**—School provides a caring, encouraging environment.

6. **Parent Involvement in Schooling**—Parent(s) are actively involved in helping young person succeed in school.

EMPOWERMENT

7. **Community Values Youth**—Young person perceives that adults in the community value youth.

8. **Youth as Resources**—Young people are given useful roles in the community.

9. **Service to Others**—Young person serves in the community one hour or more per week.

10. **Safety**—Young person feels safe at home, at school, and in the neighborhood.

BOUNDARIES AND EXPECTATIONS

11. **Family Boundaries**—Family has clear rules and consequences and monitors the young person's whereabouts.

12. **School Boundaries**—School provides clear rules and consequences.

13. **Neighborhood Boundaries**—Neighbors take responsibility for monitoring young people's behavior.

14. **Adult Role Models**—Parent(s) and other adults model positive, responsible behavior.

15. **Positive Peer Influence**—Young person's best friends model responsible behavior.

16. **High Expectations**—Both parent(s) and teachers encourage the young person to do well.

CONSTRUCTIVE USE OF TIME

17. **Creative Activitles**—Young person spends three or more hours per week in lessons or practice in music, theater, or other arts.

18. **Youth Programs**—Young person spends three or more hours per week in sports, clubs, or organizations at school and/or in the community.

19. **Religious Community**—Young person spends one or more hours per week in activities in a religious institution.

20. **Time at Home**—Young person is out with friends "with nothing special to do" two or fewer nights per week.

CONTINUES →

40 Developmental Assets for Adolescents

WITH DEFINITIONS (STUDENTS IN GRADES 6-12)

INTERNAL ASSETS

COMMITMENT TO LEARNING

21. **Achievement Motivation**—Young person is motivated to do well in school.

22. **School Engagement**—Young person is actively engaged in learning.

23. **Homework**—Young person reports doing at least one hour of homework every school day.

24. **Bonding to School**—Young person cares about her or his school.

25. **Reading for Pleasure**—Young person reads for pleasure three or more hours per week.

POSITIVE VALUES

26. **Caring**—Young person places high value on helping other people.

27. **Equality and Social Justice**—Young person places high value on promoting equality and reducing hunger and poverty.

28. **Integrity**—Young person acts on convictions and stands up for her or his beliefs.

29. **Honesty**—Young person tells the truth even when it is not easy.

30. **Responsibility**—Young person accepts and takes personal responsibility.

31. **Restraint**—Young person believes it is important not to be sexually active or to use alcohol or other drugs.

SOCIAL COMPETENCIES

32. **Planning and Decision Making**—Young person knows how to plan ahead and make choices.

33. **Interpersonal Competence**—Young person has empathy, sensitivity, and friendship skills.

34. **Cultural Competence**—Young person has knowledge of and comfort with people of different cultural/racial/ethnic backgrounds.

35. **Resistance Skills**—Young person can resist negative peer pressure and dangerous situations.

36. **Peaceful Conflict Resolution**—Young person seeks to resolve conflict nonviolently.

POSITIVE IDENTITY

37. **Personal Power**—Young person feels he or she has control over "things that happen to me."

38. **Self-Esteem**—Young person reports having a high self-esteem.

39. **Sense of Purpose**—Young person reports that "my life has a purpose."

40. **Positive View of Personal Future**—Young person is optimistic about her or his personal future.

The Power of Assets

On one level, the 40 Developmental Assets represent common wisdom about the kinds of positive experiences and characteristics that young people need and deserve. But their value extends further. Surveys of more than 2 million young people in grades 6–12 have shown that assets are powerful influences on adolescent behavior. (The numbers below reflect 2003 data from 148,189 young people in 202 communities.) Regardless of gender, ethnic heritage, economic situation, or geographic location, these assets both promote positive behaviors and attitudes and help protect young people from many different problem behaviors.

0–10 ASSETS   11–20 ASSETS   21–30 ASSETS   31–40 ASSETS

PROMOTING POSITIVE BEHAVIORS AND ATTITUDES

Search Institute research shows that the greater the number of assets students report having, the more likely they are to also report the following patterns of thriving behavior:

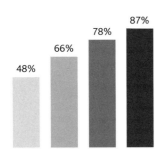

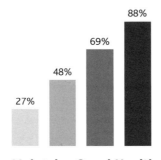

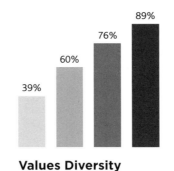

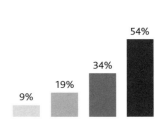

Exhibits Leadership
Has been a leader of an organization or group in the past 12 months.

Maintains Good Health
Takes good care of body (such as eating foods that are healthy and exercising regularly).

Values Diversity
Thinks it is important to get to know people of other racial/ethnic groups.

Succeeds in School
Gets mostly A's on report card (an admittedly high standard).

PROTECTING YOUTH FROM HIGH-RISK BEHAVIORS

Assets not only promote positive behaviors, they also protect young people; the more assets a young person reports having, the less likely he or she is to make harmful or unhealthy choices. (Note that high-risk behaviors are defined in terms of multiple occurrences in order to distinguish between casual experimentation and more serious, ongoing problem behaviors.)

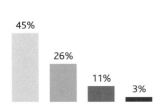

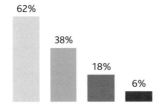

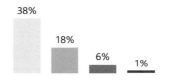

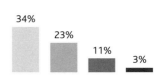

Problem Alcohol Use
Has used alcohol three or more times in the past 30 days or got drunk once or more in the past two weeks.

Violence
Has engaged in three or more acts of fighting, hitting, injuring a person, carrying a weapon, or threatening physical harm in the past 12 months.

Illicit Drug Use
Used illicit drugs (marijuana, cocaine, LSD, PCP/angel dust, heroin, or amphetamines) three or more times in the past 12 months.

Sexual Activity
Has had sexual intercourse three or more times in lifetime.

In the survey findings described above, young people reported experiencing, on average, only 19 of the 40 assets. Although it may not be likely that a young person would possess all 40 assets, the fact that the average young person experiences fewer than half should concern every community.

Mentoring programs are in an ideal position to help correct this imbalance, because they can (and do!) provide the kinds of positive relationships, places, values, and activities that build assets for and with young people. The Developmental Assets framework can also enhance the efforts of programs to provide healthy, asset-rich, nurturing environments for the youth they serve.

WHY ARE THE DEVELOPMENTAL ASSETS SO POWERFUL FOR MENTORING?

At a time when many people feel overwhelmed by the problems and challenges facing children and youth, programs are discovering new energy in working together toward a positive vision for young people. Instead of focusing solely on reducing risks and intervening in problems, these programs are rallying to build the foundation of development that all young people need by focusing on building assets through relationships, program environments, and their program's practices. In turn, taking an asset approach brings renewed enthusiasm and inspiration to staff and participants. Uniting your mentoring program to nurture the positive development of its young participants is a challenging, yet worthwhile, goal.

The assets focus on the *strengths* of young people, not their deficits. For decades, adults in our society have concentrated on identifying and "fixing" the problems that surface in youth and youth cultures. Someone observes an increase in teen pregnancy statistics and starts a program aimed at reducing teen pregnancies. We notice grades falling and set up a tutoring program. One by one, we try to patch the holes in the walls.

An asset approach, like mentoring itself, recognizes that prevention is only one element in an integrated approach that looks at what all youth need to grow up healthy. The asset framework is aimed at developing the wholeness of each young person. This approach does not ignore or downplay the critical role of prevention and intervention in addressing the risks and deficits many youth face. Instead, it highlights the strengths in and around young people that are critical to their well-being. As mentoring programs work with mentors and staff to identify and build on those strengths, the time young people spend with their mentors can become a time to "patch holes" where needed but, more important, to help create the strong and lasting foundation that all youth need.

Another empowering attribute of the Developmental Assets framework is its grounding in *relationships*. Relationships are the primary vehicle through which youth experience assets. We all learn and grow through relationships, from the care-givers who nurture us at the beginning of life to the schoolmates, colleagues, mentors, and partners who form the web of support that sustains us throughout our lives.

The asset framework emphasizes that strong relationships are essential for healthy, productive lives and makes cultivating and promoting them a priority. Mentoring programs, which are based on building relationships between mentors and mentees, provide a prime opportunity to build assets.

The asset framework also acknowledges that *everyone* can build assets for and with young people. Certainly, professional youth workers have a critical job and make important contributions to the community. However, building assets within a youth program or organization is not the job of youth workers alone. In a mentoring program, mentors—caring adults who usually are not formally trained youth development professionals—are in a unique position to provide opportunities for young people to thrive. Just as important, mentees (youth who have mentors) themselves have a responsibility to foster a positive environment. Adults will benefit from embracing them as contributors, not just passive recipients. Families, too, play a critical role in mentees' experience of assets, not only through daily care and by setting examples, but also through their support of mentors as an important part of a child's life.

The asset framework thus gives a fresh way to assess what your program is doing, what is effective, and what needs to be improved. Looking at your work through an asset lens helps you see opportunities to do what you already do better and lends clarity as you consider what you want to alter or enhance in your mentoring program.

WHAT THIS BOOK OFFERS

The purpose of this publication is to furnish mentoring professionals with accessible tools to enhance the quality of mentoring relationships. Whether you are new to the mentoring field or a seasoned professional, this publication can offer guidance and tips to make the mentoring relationships you support all they can be. Mentoring matches that are struggling can find insight in a Developmental Assets approach to mentoring to help them identify strengths and opportunities. At the same time, matches that are already thriving will find new ideas to take their relationships to the next level. The handouts for mentors are relevant for mentors of all ages, from teenage peer mentors to senior citizens. The content of all handouts is intended for work with mentees between the ages of 10 and 18.

A unique feature of this publication is that it includes resources for the families of mentees. Although we sometimes use the phrase "parents and caregivers," the information is relevant for anyone playing a parental role for a mentee, including grandparents, older siblings, and other types of guardians. The reason for addressing this audience is simple: Families can be an important part of the mentoring team, and the better equipped they are to support their child's mentoring relationship, the better. Research shows that when families provide support to the mentor and mentee, they increase the chances that the mentoring relationship will flourish.[3] And mentoring relationships can help parents and caregivers be more effective, since supportive mentors can reinforce their boundaries and positive values.

This book is for anyone who is helping mentors and mentees build and sustain meaningful, nurturing relationships, while also encouraging families of mentees to support their child's relationship with their mentor. The ideas and advice compiled in this book come from mentors, former mentors, and mentoring program professionals who have spent years supporting mentoring matches. Like you, all of these contributors are keenly aware of two very important realities about mentoring:

- At its best, a successful mentoring relationship can provide a young person with critical support and opportunities for growth that he or she may not be receiving in life. As professionals in the field of mentoring, you are in a unique position to work with mentors, mentees, and mentees' families to help young people thrive.

- Unsuccessful mentoring relationships can have distressing impacts on mentees and their families.[4] For this reason, it is crucial that mentoring professionals are equipped with multiple tools to help relationships between mentors and mentees succeed.

The research behind the Developmental Assets can also assist you in making the case for your program and give leadership and staff a context for talking with community leaders and funders about what you do, why you do it, how your efforts are effective, and why they matter. In addition, the framework uses a common language that assures youth receive the asset message from everyone in your organization.

By examining the roles of program staff, mentors, mentees, and mentees' families, we see how each person can contribute to a successful mentoring relationship. No doubt your program already has its own policies and practices; this is not a suggestion to implement a new program. Instead, this book allows you to enhance the good work you are already doing and to select the handouts that best serve the people in *your* mentoring setting.

HOW TO GET THE MOST OUT OF THIS BOOK

Each of the handouts in *Mentoring for Meaningful Results* can be reproduced and distributed to program leaders, mentors, mentees, or the families of mentees. Many handouts work well for mentor trainings or advance preparation of mentees and their families. Consider making copies of several of the handouts and placing them in a high-traffic area with other free resources.

You can also use these handouts on a more individual basis. Imagine a nervous new mentor who is unclear about her or his role in the mentoring relationship. Consider giving the mentor handout 8, which addresses this issue. For all mentors, mentees, or parents and caregivers new to the 40 Developmental Assets, you can use the lists of assets (pages 8–11) or the corresponding handout to introduce each audience to the framework.

You can use these handouts in a variety of mentoring settings. Some of the content works especially well for community-based mentoring, in which mentors and mentees are meeting outside of school, congregation, residential, or programmatic settings. However, participants in all kinds of mentoring programs—including those with group mentors or teen mentors of younger kids—will find helpful advice they can adapt for their unique situations.

Although the handouts for mentors, mentees, and parents can be useful tools for supporting mentoring relationships that are already active, nothing can replace effective recruiting, screening, matching, training, and ongoing support from your program as the primary means to ensure that a mentoring match has the strongest chances of flourishing. The first section of handouts in this resource offers program leaders tools for establishing these effective "up front" infrastructures that position a mentoring relationship for success. You may already have a solid process in place, but this section can help inform and enhance your existing strategies.

MOVING FORWARD

Effective mentoring programs build a strong team composed of a mentor, mentee, and the mentee's family, with program staff offering coaching and support along the way. The concepts and language of the Developmental Assets framework can make mentors feel more equipped and empowered to make a difference. In addition, the asset approach can help mentees understand the gifts and talents they have to offer the world and help parents see easy, doable ways in which they can guide their children toward a healthy future. For mentoring programs, the Developmental Assets can provide the framework and language to unite the mentoring team around a truly meaningful result—helping young people thrive.

NOTES

1. Scales, Peter C., and Leffert, Nancy. (2004). *Developmental Assets: A Synthesis of the Scientific Research on Adolescent Development*, 2d ed. (Minneapolis: Search Institute).

2. Scales, Peter C., Sesma, Arturo, Jr., and Bolstrom, Brent. (2004). *Coming into Their Own: How Developmental Assets Promote Positive Growth in Middle Childhood* (Minneapolis: Search Institute).

3. Rhodes, J. E., Grossman, J. B., and Resch, N. L. (2000). Agents of Change: Pathways through Which Mentoring Relationships Influence Adolescents' Academic Adjustment. *Child Development, 71* (6), 1662–1671.

4. Grossman, J. B., and Rhodes, J. E. (2002). The Test of Time: Predictors and Effects of Duration in Youth Mentoring Relationships. *American Journal of Community Psychology, 30* (2), 199–219.

MENTORING PROGRAM PROVIDERS

As a mentoring professional you know that your work, when done well, can make a positive difference in the lives of young people, their families, and their mentors. But you may wonder: Are we doing enough? Could we do more to support effective mentoring experiences—without seeking additional funding or staff?

With any job, *how* you do the tasks is as important as *what* you do. Being a mentoring program provider is no different. The handouts in this section present a variety of ideas for *how* you can use the Developmental Assets framework to examine your strengths and improve upon your existing practices. This section begins with introductory information about assets, then takes program providers from recruitment through match support, showing how you can foster the development of caring, healthy, and responsible young people at every stage. By reminding your staff people to think of each other, mentors, mentees, and the families of mentees as members of the same team, you can begin to build the web of support that helps young people thrive. Use these handouts to be sure your staff learns how to purposefully integrate asset-based strategies into your program.

These handouts are not "recipes" for an ideal asset-building mentoring program. Rather, the ideas offered here can complement your current strategies and help you identify opportunities to incorporate the principles of asset building more intentionally. You may find it helpful to start by asking yourself:

- What are the best strengths I bring to my role in supporting mentor–mentee matches?

- In my role, how can I most effectively leverage those strengths in our mentoring organization?

- How can other staff in our program share their talents as asset builders?

Understanding each person's role as an asset builder will help your staff send consistent messages to program participants. Once your staff learns to unleash the power of this positive approach, you'll be ready to continue your journey toward even more meaningful results for mentors, mentees, and mentees' families.

1

What Are Developmental Assets?

You have decided to work in mentoring at least in part because you want to make a positive difference in the lives of young people. Whether you realize it or not, you are in a fantastic position to help young people attain the experiences and qualities they need to be successful. Search Institute, a nonprofit research organization based in Minneapolis, Minnesota, uses a framework of 40 Developmental Assets to describe what youth need to grow into caring, responsible adults. (If you haven't already received a copy of the complete list, please visit www.search-institute.org/assets/assetlists to learn more.)

You can think about assets as "nutrients" that are necessary for a child to grow a strong mind and character. Knowing more about Developmental Assets can equip you to build an even more meaningful mentoring program, because the list can help you give mentors tools and ideas for building on the strengths of mentees and helping them overcome difficulties.

Simply but powerfully, assets build the "good stuff" in kids and help them resist the "bad stuff." Research has shown that the more assets young people have, the more likely they are to be leaders in their community, succeed in school, and maintain good health—all outcomes we want for kids. Just as important, the more assets young people have, the more likely they are to resist risky behavior, such as using alcohol or other drugs, skipping school, or fighting.

Assets don't just happen as part of growing up. They are built for and with children through all of the caring relationships they have at home and in their communities. Family members, mentors, teachers, coaches, youth directors, neighbors, and employers all have opportunities to help young people be stronger.

The 40 assets are grouped into two main types: external and internal assets. The external assets are the good qualities of life young people get from the world around them. The internal assets are the traits, behaviors, and values that help kids make positive choices and be better prepared for challenging situations. Internal assets are like the internal compass that helps guide them. These two types of assets are divided into eight categories of human development that make it easier to think about activities to build them.

CONTINUES →

WHAT ARE DEVELOPMENTAL ASSETS? **1**

EXTERNAL ASSETS

SUPPORT is about youth having people and places that make them feel cared about and welcome. Encourage mentors to think about contributing to a web of support for young people that includes family members, nonfamily adults, and caring schools and neighborhoods.

EMPOWERMENT is about young people feeling valued for who they are and being given opportunities to shine. It's also about feeling safe, because it's tough to be your best if you feel scared. You can model this for mentors by describing mentees as equal contributors to, rather than passive recipients of, your program's services.

BOUNDARIES AND EXPECTATIONS are about knowing and understanding the rules of behavior in families, schools, and communities. This category is also about adults and peers encouraging young people to be their best. You can help mentors and mentees set responsible ground rules. Try to reward mentees for positive words and actions, but also work with mentors to plan reasonable consequences for behaviors that are not acceptable within your program.

CONSTRUCTIVE USE OF TIME is about young people having people *and* activities in their lives that are fun and challenging. It is also about having high-quality time at home. Help mentors provide mentees with opportunities to experience constructive use of time through a balance of creative activities, youth programs, involvement in faith communities, and time at home with family members.

INTERNAL ASSETS

COMMITMENT TO LEARNING is about doing well in school, but it is also about taking advantage of all opportunities to learn whenever they happen. Encourage mentors and mentees to spend time learning new things, setting goals at school, completing homework assignments, and reading for pleasure.

POSITIVE VALUES define who young people are and how they interact with others. Suggest that mentors and mentees spend time talking about positive values such as integrity, honesty, and responsibility.

SOCIAL COMPETENCIES are about getting along with all kinds of people and being able to navigate through the rough waters of decision making in today's society. Offer role-playing exercises or other tools to help mentors and mentees practice social competencies such as planning and decision making, interpersonal skills, and peaceful conflict resolution.

POSITIVE IDENTITY is about youth feeling good about themselves and knowing they can succeed in life. It's about looking forward to the future. Work with mentors to champion young people by building their self-esteem, sense of purpose, and personal view of the future.

2

An Asset-Building Checklist for Mentoring Organizations

Think of Developmental Assets as salt in the ocean or oxygen in blood. Asset-building opportunities should permeate the life of a young person, and likewise, the Developmental Assets need to be infused throughout a mentoring program. Use this checklist to see how you're currently building Developmental Assets and to identify areas you could strengthen.

	WE ALREADY DO THIS WELL	WE COULD DO THIS BETTER	NOT SURE WE CAN DO THIS
SUPPORT			
Does our program aim to be part of a larger web of support that includes mentees' families, schools, and neighborhoods?	☐	☐	☐
Do we communicate with mentors, mentees, and mentees' families to recognize the important roles they each play in supporting the mentoring relationship?	☐	☐	☐
EMPOWERMENT			
Does our training and recruitment process reflect that we appreciate young people as valuable participants with something to contribute, not just as "needing our help"?	☐	☐	☐
Do we conduct background checks or take other measures to make our program as safe as possible?	☐	☐	☐
BOUNDARIES AND EXPECTATIONS			
Do we set clear, consistent boundaries for behavior in our program?	☐	☐	☐
Do we have high expectations and reward the positive behavior we see?	☐	☐	☐

CONTINUES →

	WE ALREADY DO THIS WELL	WE COULD DO THIS BETTER	NOT SURE WE CAN DO THIS
CONSTRUCTIVE USE OF TIME			
Do we encourage our program's participants to balance their involvement with other important activities?	☐	☐	☐
Do we offer mentors and mentees opportunities to take part in a variety of creative activities?	☐	☐	☐
COMMITMENT TO LEARNING			
Does our program motivate mentees to do well in school?	☐	☐	☐
Do our mentors and mentees spend time learning new things, completing homework assignments, or reading for pleasure?	☐	☐	☐
POSITIVE VALUES			
Have we identified all the ways our programs may affect or engage *all* young people, regardless of gender, ability, race, ethnicity, culture, sexual orientation, or socioeconomic status?	☐	☐	☐
Does our program staff articulate the values that are important to our organization?	☐	☐	☐
SOCIAL COMPETENCIES			
Do we provide mentors and mentees with tools for building strong, positive relationships?	☐	☐	☐
Do we have policies and resources to help mentors and mentees practice peaceful conflict resolution?	☐	☐	☐
POSITIVE IDENTITY			
Do the adults in our program share power and work *with* young people instead of doing things *for* them?	☐	☐	☐
Does our program help young people plan for the future?	☐	☐	☐

After you have completed this worksheet, use it as a discussion starter. What are your current asset-building strengths? How can you build on the things that are already working well? What are your areas of opportunity? Which things are you unable to do, given the structure, nature, or mission of your organization? How can this checklist help you in making plans and developing ways to act?

3

What's Different about Mentoring Programs That Build Assets?

When mentoring programs adopt an asset-building perspective, it can affect many things about the way they work with mentors, mentees, and families. Here are some of the aspects that may change.

MENTORING MYTHS	AN ASSET-BUILDING APPROACH TO MENTORING
Mentors are "substitute parents."	Mentors and families are on the same team.
One caring adult is all a young person needs.	Young people benefit from positive relationships with *many* caring adults.
Only formal, one-on-one mentoring matters.	Effective mentoring can happen in both informal and group settings.
All mentoring relationships are equal.	Mentors and mentees can have even more meaningful relationships by building assets together.
It's often unclear what actions and activities in the program actually make a difference in the lives of youth.	The research-based framework names concrete things the program can do to make a lasting difference for youth.
Mentors are recruited to be "saviors" for youth who are "at risk."	Mentors are recruited to engage in positive relationships with young people who have the potential for great things.
Mentors are in charge of selecting activities to do with the mentee.	Mentors and mentees jointly select activities to do together.
Mentors give advice and build skills; mentees are recipients of their help.	Mentors help mentees see that they have gifts and talents to share with their mentors and their community.
Families are only superficially involved in the mentoring program and are consulted primarily when behavioral issues arise.	Families are active partners in shaping the program and are supported by the program in their roles as parents or caregivers.
The program operates as a separate entity with little or no connection to other community organizations and institutions serving youth and their families.	The program views itself as a part of a web of community support for youth and is connected in formal and informal ways with other organizations and institutions serving youth and their families.

4

Incorporating Asset-Building Strategies into Mentor Recruitment

Developmental Assets are positive factors within young people, families, schools, and other settings that have been found to be important in promoting young people's development. Incorporating asset-building language and principles into your mentor recruitment process can help you frame the role of a mentor in a way that encourages potential mentors. Below are ways to consider using the concepts inherent in the Developmental Assets framework to enhance your recruitment strategies.

MARKETING

How you portray mentors and mentees in your program's marketing can determine how people perceive what mentors are—and are not. Some hints:

- When recruiting mentors, make sure to use marketing materials and handouts that depict young people with promise and potential, rather than just with problems that need fixing.

- Portray mentors as friends and role models who can bring out the best in a young person, not as rescuers or problem fixers.

- Use images and anecdotes that reflect mentors and mentees with diverse characteristics and experiences. Focus on positive possibilities rather than deficits.

PRESENTATIONS

When making presentations to potential mentors, whether in a group setting or a one-on-one meeting, remember to incorporate the following messages:

- Think back on the adults outside your family who made a difference for you when you were growing up. Who were those adults? What did they do to make you feel special? Mentors need not have a degree in youth development to make a difference. They just need to believe in the potential of a young person.

- Relationships, not programs, build healthy young people. Mentoring programs are about sparking and supporting relationships between young people and adults.

- Remember that the little things *are* the big things. A mentor may never have a dramatic, life-changing conversation with a young person like you see in the movies. However, the accumulation of everyday interactions—doing homework together, laughing over ice cream, shooting hoops, or talking during a bus ride—gradually builds the foundation upon which mentors can help young people thrive.

- All young people have the potential to grow, and having a caring relationship with a nonfamily adult is one key way young people find the means to flourish.

- Mentees aren't just recipients of mentors' caring and affection. They may have just as much to offer and teach as adults do. Mentoring benefits mentors as well as mentees.

5

Incorporating Asset-Building Strategies into Mentor Screening

Once you have recruited a potential mentor into the screening phase, the Developmental Assets framework can act as a guide for getting to know more about the potential mentor's style for interacting with young people. Equally important, the way you ask questions and present program requirements using the asset framework helps potential mentors sense the kind of mentor you expect them to be. Below are some tips for ensuring that your message comes across.

INTERVIEWING

Once a potential mentor has signed on to proceed through the screening process, there are ways that you can look for their existing asset-building tendencies and build on those strengths. In your interviewing of mentors, ask the following questions:

- When you think of young people, what comes to mind? (Look for people with a natural tendency to view young people as having the potential to succeed.)

- What would you see as your role in the mentoring relationship? (Look for responses that indicate that this person would be open to both supporting a young person and to growing as an individual through the experience of mentoring. Too much emphasis on only one of these interests could be problematic.)

- How do you currently interact with young people you encounter in your daily life? (Look for people who say they try to say hello and engage in conversation with young people.)

"JOB" DESCRIPTIONS

Give potential mentors a written description of the expectations your program has of mentors. Use the asset categories in your descriptions.

- Provide support to mentees by being there during tough times and celebrating their successes.

- Empower mentees to be full partners in the relationship by sharing responsibility for choosing activities you do together.

- Believe in young people and their ability to make a difference in the world.

- Have high expectations for the behavior and achievement of mentees. Set fair but clear boundaries for how they should behave.

- Engage mentees in a rich array of activities, from just hanging out to trying creative new experiences.

- Foster mentees' commitment to learning. Connect their real-world interests to academics.

- Model positive values through your priorities and choices.

- Help mentees hone positive values and social competencies, such as honesty, integrity, and respecting people who are different from them.

- Be a trustworthy adult. Maintain confidentiality whenever possible, and help mentees seek outside help when necessary.

- Remind mentees of their purpose, worth, and promise.

6

Incorporating Asset-Building Strategies into Orientation and Training

Both mentors and mentees can benefit when you incorporate asset-building information, ideas, and strategies into orientations and ongoing trainings. Launching the mentoring relationship on the right foot can help ensure the relationship is grounded in an environment of thriving and growing, rather than one of bridging differences and problem solving.

IN GENERAL

- Introduce the Developmental Assets framework during orientation sessions for mentors and mentees. Explain that good mentoring builds assets in young people—and good mentoring requires both mentors and mentees to understand what they need to do to make the relationship a success.

- Find ways to reinforce with both mentors and mentees in ongoing training what asset building is (intentionally creating the opportunities and experiences described in the framework), why asset building matters (the more assets young people have, the more likely they are to grow into healthy, caring, and responsible young adults), and how people build assets (through relationships with family, friends, and other caring adults).

- If mentees and/or mentors are given orientation in a group setting, use the activity called "Building a Web of Support" at the end of this handout to demonstrate what asset building is.

- Consider using the Developmental Assets framework (either the individual assets themselves or the eight asset categories) as a series of topics for developing and providing ongoing training and support opportunities with mentors and mentees.

ASSET-BUILDING ORIENTATION AND TRAINING FOR MENTEES

Obviously, a mentee orientation should help young people understand the "nuts and bolts" of a mentoring relationship, such as who their mentors are, what they can expect will happen during visits, and how often they will spend time with their mentors. The orientation is also a great opportunity to introduce mentees to the concept of Developmental Assets.

Below are some ideas for how to introduce asset building to mentees:

- During orientation, address the following topics with mentees:
  - My Mentor's Role in My Life
  - What Are Developmental Assets?
  - Conversation Topics for Introducing Yourselves
  - Deeper Conversation Topics
  - (See additional handouts in *Mentoring for Meaningful Results: Asset-Building Tips, Tools, and Activities for Youth and Adults,* copyright © 2006, Search Institute.)

- When talking to mentees about why they are enrolled in a mentoring program, give them the following kinds of messages:

CONTINUES →

– There are adults—parents or guardians, the program staff, your new mentor—who believe in you. Having another adult friend can help you become even more responsible, happy, and confident than you already are.

– Sometimes having another adult friend in your life can give you someone else to talk to and do things with —and who doesn't need supportive friends?

■ At the orientation and ongoing trainings offered to mentees, remind mentees that they are important players in the direction of their own life, and that they have a role in making their own lives—and the lives of others—the best they can be.

ASSET-BUILDING ORIENTATION AND TRAINING FOR MENTORS

In addition to the specific details you need to give mentors in orientation sessions (such as how often they should meet with their mentees and rules regarding proper and improper conduct), asset-building information and messages can give new mentors a firm foundation for positive interactions with their mentees.

■ During orientation, address the following topics with mentors:

– Frequently Asked Questions about Being a Mentor

– What Is My Role as a Mentor?

– What Are Developmental Assets?

– What Is Asset Building?

– Conversation Topics for Introducing Yourselves

– Deeper Conversation Topics

– (See additional handouts in *Mentoring for Meaningful Results: Asset-Building Tips, Tools, and Activities for Youth and Adults,* copyright © 2006, Search Institute.)

■ Incorporate the following messages into mentor orientation and any ongoing training:

– Mentors provide another source of support in the lives of their mentees to help them gain the confidence to reach their full potential in life.

– Every young person has strengths and talents to build on; mentors should affirm their mentees' strengths and expand their horizons to discover new interests and skills.

■ At the orientation and ongoing training, remind mentors that strong relationships build assets, and their focus should be on building and maintaining the trust and camaraderie of the relationship as a foundation on which other aspects of the relationship can be supported.

For more information on other Search Institute resources that can augment your program's orientation and training session, visit www.search-

CONTINUES →

BUILDING A WEB OF SUPPORT

For this exercise, you will need:

- A beach ball, balloon, or other type of lightweight ball

- A ball of yarn (enough to make a web among several people)

INSTRUCTIONS

1 Have your group stand or sit in a circle. Give one person a ball of yarn. Have that person name one person who has supported her or him and describe how.

2 Ask that person to hold on to the end of the yarn and throw the rest of the ball to another person in the circle.

3 The person who catches the ball of yarn then names a person who has supported her or him and describes how, before holding on to the yarn at that point and throwing the ball to someone else.

4 As the activity continues, a web will form that connects all the people in the circle. Make sure everyone gets to participate at least once.

5 After a web has been spun and the people in the circle begin to run out of ideas, explain to them that the ball represents young people and the crisscrossing yarn is the web of support made up of all of the people mentioned and the asset-building actions they have taken.

6 Throw the ball into the web and encourage the group to move it around without letting it slip through the gaps in the web. If the web cannot support the ball, continue adding to it until the ball bounces easily without falling through.

7 Stop and ask these questions:

- How many different types of people did we name (e.g., family, friends, neighbors)?

- Is it more important to you to have lots of different people who are supportive or just a few who are very supportive? Why?

- What happens when the gaps in our webs of support are too wide?

- Which attributes do supportive people have that are important to you?

- In what ways do you support your friends and family?

- If someone you know seems to need more support, how would you suggest that he or she find it?

7

Incorporating Asset-Building Strategies into Match Support

Whether or not the Developmental Assets were introduced directly to mentors and mentees in your program orientation, the framework can still provide matches with helpful guidance on where to focus their energy and how to approach issues that arise. Ultimately, the Developmental Assets serve as a strong reminder of why they're in this relationship in the first place.

There are plenty of ways you can intentionally incorporate asset-building advice and tips into your staff's match support efforts. Some ideas include:

- Share handouts from *Mentoring for Meaningful Results: Asset-Building Tips, Tools, and Activities for Youth and Adults* or other asset-building materials to help mentors and mentees think about situations from an asset-building perspective.

- Remember that mentoring should be about helping mentees be all they can be, rather than about fixing mentees' problems. Focusing on what's right with a young person is key to how you frame your support strategies.

- Never forget the power of affirmation. The more mentors and mentees hear genuine praise for their efforts, the more motivated they will be to stick with the program during any tough times that may arise.

- Remind mentors and mentees that no one is expecting perfection. Rather, the hope is that mentees and mentors will put forth their best efforts to reach out to each other, to model appropriate behavior, to admit when they've made a mistake, and to be willing to forgive.

- Use the Developmental Assets framework to shape questions you have for mentees and mentors during match support conversations. For example, to learn more about how mentors provide support in the relationship, you could ask the mentor, "What strategies have you been using to show your mentee your support?" Mentees could be asked, "When your mentor shows that he or she supports you, how do you know it? What does he or she say or do?"

MENTORS

People unfamiliar with mentoring may assume that, as long as mentors care about their mentees and spend time with them, the relationship will yield positive outcomes for mentees. As a mentoring professional, you know that mentoring is much more complex than that. For example, *how* a mentor engages with her or his mentee is just as important as *how often*. Equipping mentors to build healthy relationships with mentees is one of the most crucial roles you play as a program provider.

The following section gives mentors information, tips, and concrete ideas for making the most of their time with their mentees. These handouts will provide you with a rich supply of helpful tools to offer mentors as they learn about mentoring and encounter challenges. This section continues to use the Developmental Assets framework as a lens through which to look at common mentoring issues. The advice focuses not just on addressing "problems" but also on recognizing the mentor's many opportunities to foster mentee development in the process.

Chances are, you are already well aware of how valuable mentors can be as agents of positive youth development. Use this information to channel their enthusiasm toward even more meaningful mentoring results.

8

What Is My Role as a Mentor?

It seems simple at first, the notion of being a mentor: someone who spends time with a young person. But once you are in the mentor role, you may find yourself in situations where you are uncertain about your part in the relationship. Is it appropriate to provide discipline when she's out of line? What if I suspect he is experiencing trouble at home—what is my responsibility? How can I have the most positive impact on my mentee?

There is no one answer concerning what your role is or is not. If you are involved in a formal mentoring program, the staff may be able to provide clearer direction for you based on the program's rules and expectations. In general, here are some basic guidelines to help you determine your role with your mentee.

YOU ARE . . .

. . . a friend. Like peer friendships, mentors and mentees do things together that are fun and engaging. They support each other both in good times and in tough times. They teach each other. They help each other. They're honest with each other. And sometimes they have to have hard conversations about concerns they have, asking the right questions at the right time. By being a good listener and engaging in authentic conversations with your mentee, you are helping her develop important life skills.

. . . a role model. You are expected to set a good example to the mentee for how to live your life. This is not the same as being perfect. Rather, it is about acknowledging your imperfections and sharing your strengths. It is also about advocating for your mentee when dangers to his physical or emotional well-being are present.

. . . a confidant. Building a close relationship with your mentee will help her build better relationships with others in her life as well, such as parents and peers. In the process, your mentee may tell you things she does not feel comfortable telling anyone else. Sometimes she may tell you about her hopes, dreams, or insecurities. Other times she may reveal mistakes she has made. Unless your mentee is in trouble and needs outside help, try to keep her private comments between the two of you. Your role is to be supportive of your mentee as a person with potential, regardless of the kinds of actions or attitudes she confides in you.

. . . a nurturer of possibilities. Your role is to see the gifts and strengths of your mentee and help him flourish personally. You should help your mentee channel his gifts toward actions that make him a resource to others in his family, neighborhood, school, or community.

CONTINUES →

YOU ARE NOT . . .

. . . a mentor to the family. In fact, some mentoring programs intentionally limit contact between mentors and parents. Your role is to provide special attention to your mentee. While getting acquainted with parents, caregivers, and siblings can be helpful to understanding your mentee and her situation, your energy and attention should be focused on providing support to your mentee.

. . . a social worker or doctor. If your mentee tells you about experiences or health conditions that concern you, always turn to the mentoring program staff for help. Although arming yourself with information about, say, a learning disability or abuse may help you understand your mentee better, it is not your responsibility to try to address conditions or situations that require professional help. The staff at the mentoring program may be able to find additional help for the mentee, including local information and referral services.

. . . a savior. You should not see your role in this relationship as coming in to make a young person's life better or to fix his problems. Certainly your support can help your mentee overcome hurdles. But don't forget that every young person—regardless of his circumstances—has gifts and talents that make him more than a "recipient" of your support. Your mentee should be treated as having much to offer to the world, because he does.

9

Frequently Asked Questions about Being a Mentor

As you think about embarking on a new mentoring relationship, you may feel nervous or unsure about some aspects of this new friendship. You're not alone! Even experienced mentors will encounter bumps in the road, and nobody has all the answers.

Your mentoring program may have several resources to help you make introductions, plan activities, and handle conflicts. Below are several common questions that arise in mentoring programs, but be sure to seek additional information from the staff at your program.

❶ Won't young people and their parents be leery of a stranger like me trying to be their friend?

It's possible. And of course, many young people are taught to beware of all strangers. But remember, nobody expects you to burst into someone's home and announce, "Here I am, your brand-new friend!" Just as you would in any friendship, you'll need to spend some time earning trust. Your mentoring program probably has guidelines about spending time with mentees and communicating with their families. Ask a staff person for help in starting the relationship off on the right foot. Mentoring relationships that receive family support have an even greater chance of being successful.

❷ Young people's problems are so complex. What can I possibly do?

Remember, you have an impact on young people even if you don't interact with them—through role modeling, for example—but you're more likely to have a positive impact if you try to be a positive influence. Many young people are lonely and could benefit from the friendship of a caring adult. In one study by the World Health Organization during the 1997–1998 school year, nearly 20 percent of 15-year-olds in the United States reported feeling lonely.

And think about it for a minute—put yourself in a young person's shoes. Even if you were a teen who was coping with depression, substance abuse, or an eating disorder, and even if you saw a number of specialists for these problems, you would still need adult friends in your life, right? You would still need people with whom you could share ideas, go to a movie, laugh over an embarrassing moment, or talk with about future plans. So, try not to think of yourself as a problem fixer. Although you may have more life experience than a young person's peers, you can consider yourself a friend—that's all, and that's plenty.

❸ Young people and I are so different from each other. How can we be friends?

If you feel intimidated by the "cultural" gaps in the modern world—differences that arise from race, age, generation, language, ability, education level, wealth—imagine what it's like for someone who's barely into her or his second decade of life. Remember that you and your mentee are strangers to one another at first; he or she may be feeling a little awkward or uncomfortable, too. But if you take a second look at the situation, maybe you'll be comforted by the idea that *discomfort* is something you and your mentee have in common.

CONTINUES →

Realize that you're both starting from the same place, but as an adult you have the benefit of a few extra years of experience, and maybe more confidence. Look beyond the surface. Allow yourself to be curious and to learn. Don't think you have to be an expert in the latest music, slang, clothes, or piercing trends to make a connection with a young person. In fact, that's not what most young people want; they want you to be a grown-up, but a grown-up who connects with them and looks for common ground with them. You don't have to be the same as one another; but as you explore similarities and differences, your mutual understanding will fill the gaps and form a friendship bond that lasts.

❹ I'm not exactly "cool." What if my mentee doesn't like me?

Don't worry. Most young people don't *expect* you to be cool, and they can like you without *being* like you. What's more important to them is that you be authentic. They'd much rather you be yourself, complete with all your quirks and imperfections, than keep your distance for fear of being thought uncool. If you can show sincere interest in young people as unique human beings with gifts to be discovered—as people who deserve to be respected and supported—that's really all it takes. You'll be surprised how fast you connect with your mentee when you genuinely take an interest in who they are.

❺ What if my mentee won't talk to me?

Shyness is especially common at the beginning of a relationship, but even prolonged silence is not necessarily an indication that you're not connecting. Some young people will simply enjoy your company without saying much about it. Silence is okay, and you might learn to feel more comfortable with it if you discover that your mentee is just a quiet person.

When you begin talking with your mentee, try to avoid bombarding her or him with lots of questions that require a yes or no response. Instead, use open-ended questions and share anecdotes about your own feelings and experiences. By stopping to ask, "Can you think of anything that made you feel the same way?" or "Do you have any advice for me?" you can build trust and identify similarities between the two of you.

❻ What if I say the wrong thing?

Mentors are not perfect. Just like any other human being, you may find yourself saying something embarrassing, hurtful, or even offensive to your mentee. When you realize that you've made a mistake, you can use the opportunity to model humility. Offer a heartfelt apology. Admit you were wrong. You may be the first adult who has ever shown your young friend this type of respect by asking for forgiveness. Seeing adults handle problems and take responsibility can help youth develop their own positive conflict resolution skills.

❼ What kinds of things will my mentee and I do together?

Mentoring programs vary widely. You may be participating in a one-on-one mentoring program that meets in a school cafeteria, a group mentoring program organized by a juvenile justice organization, or an informal mentoring club started by a congregation. Depending on the location and boundaries set by your specific program, you may have preplanned activities or a range of options.

Talk with program staff to learn which activities are appropriate in your setting. You and your mentee may do homework assignments, or you may conduct service projects for a local charity, or you may play card games, or you may occasionally just run errands together. The important thing is not *what* you do, but *how* you do it. Make it clear that friendship and learning more about each other are the main goals.

CONTINUES →

❽ What will I do if my mentee tells me something I'm not sure how to handle (e.g., he's afraid to tell his parents he is gay, she's being bullied at school, his girlfriend is pregnant)?

When you build trust with a young person, you may find that you hear intimate, unexpected, and even shocking or upsetting revelations. As a mentor, your job is to listen, to avoid being judgmental, and to defer to program staff or other professionals when you know that a mentee needs help. Before you find yourself in a situation like this, it is helpful to define ground rules for confidentiality. Early on in your relationship, you and your mentee can talk about what you expect from each other. Explain that you will be an open listener, but you will always try to do what is best for your young friend. Talk generally about physical and emotional health and safety issues that might require help from other people. Assure your mentee that you will always act with her or his best interests in mind. If there comes a time when you need to seek outside help for your mentee, you can refer back to the promises you made in this early conversation.

10

What Are Developmental Assets?

You have become a mentor at least in part because you want to make a positive difference in the life of a young person. Many of the small and big things you do to make that difference are included in a comprehensive list called the Developmental Assets framework. The framework is made up of 40 commonsense, positive experiences and qualities that young people need to be successful. (If you haven't received a copy of the complete list, please visit www.search-institute.org/assets/assetlists to learn more.)

You can think about assets as "nutrients" that are necessary for a child to grow a strong mind and character. Knowing more about Developmental Assets can equip you to be an even more effective mentor, because the framework gives mentors tools and ideas for building on the strengths of mentees and helping them overcome difficulties and become caring, responsible adults.

Simply but powerfully, assets build the "good stuff" in kids and help them resist the "bad stuff." Research done by Search Institute, a nonprofit research organization based in Minneapolis, Minnesota, has shown that the more assets young people have, the more likely they are to be leaders in their community, succeed in school, and maintain good health—all outcomes we want for kids. Just as important, the more assets young people have, the more likely they are to resist risky behaviors, such as using alcohol or other drugs, skipping school, or fighting.

Assets don't just happen as part of growing up. They are built for and with children through all of the caring relationships they have at home and in their communities. Family members, mentors, teachers, coaches, youth directors, neighbors, and employers all have opportunities to help young people be stronger.

The 40 assets are grouped into two main types: external and internal assets. The external assets are the good qualities of life young people get from the world around them. The internal assets are the traits, behaviors, and values that help kids make positive choices and be better prepared for challenging situations. Internal assets are like the internal compass that helps guide them. These two types of assets are divided into eight categories of human development that make it easier to think about activities to build them.

CONTINUES →

EXTERNAL ASSETS

SUPPORT is about youth having people and places that make them feel cared about and welcome. Think about providing your mentee with opportunities to experience support from numerous nonfamily adults, positive family communication, and a caring neighborhood.

EMPOWERMENT is about young people feeling valued for who they are and being given opportunities to shine. It's also about feeling safe, because it's tough to be your best if you feel scared. Think about ways you can provide your mentee with opportunities to experience empowerment by being in a safe environment and providing service to others.

BOUNDARIES AND EXPECTATIONS are about knowing and understanding the rules of behavior in families, schools, and communities. This category is also about adults and peers encouraging young people to be their best. Think about ways you can provide your mentee with opportunities to experience boundaries and expectations through adult role models, family, positive peer influences, and high expectations.

CONSTRUCTIVE USE OF TIME is about youth having people and activities in their lives that are fun *and* challenging. It is also about having high-quality time at home. Think about ways you can provide your mentee with opportunities to experience constructive use of time through creative activities, religious community, and time at home.

INTERNAL ASSETS

COMMITMENT TO LEARNING is about doing well in school, but it is also about taking advantage of all opportunities to learn whenever they happen. Think about ways you can provide your mentee with opportunities to experience a commitment to learning through achievement motivation, doing homework, and reading for pleasure.

POSITIVE VALUES define who young people are and how they interact with others. Think about ways you can provide your mentee with opportunities to experience positive values such as integrity, honesty, and responsibility.

SOCIAL COMPETENCIES are about getting along with all kinds of people and being able to navigate through the rough waters of decision making in today's society. Think about ways you can provide your mentee with opportunities to experience social competencies such as friendship skills and peaceful conflict resolution.

POSITIVE IDENTITY is about youth feeling good about themselves and knowing they can succeed in life. It's about looking forward to the future. Think about ways you can provide your mentee with opportunities to experience positive identity by building her or his self-esteem, sense of purpose, and personal view of the future.

11

What Is Asset Building?

What kind of difference can one mentor realistically make in the life of a mentee? There is no simple answer to this question. Search Institute, a nonprofit organization whose mission is to provide leadership, knowledge, and resources to promote healthy children, youth, and communities, offers some basic guidance for anyone who wants to make a difference in the lives of young people.

Search Institute has identified a list of 40 Developmental Assets that fall into eight categories; the list describes the kinds of experiences, skills, and opportunities that matter in the healthy development of young people. (If you have not already received other information about the 40 Developmental Assets, please visit www.search-institute. org/assets to learn more.)

Key Principles of Asset Building

Below are some general principles you can use to help your mentee (or any young person in your life) successfully build Developmental Assets.

- **Everyone can help young people build assets**—not just parents, teachers, and people with college degrees in child and youth development. Whether you are an electrician or a singer, you have the power to be a positive influence in the life of a young person.

- **All young people need assets.** Search Institute's research shows that almost all young people need more assets than they have. Young people may have lots of friends or achieve high marks in school, but they may be lacking in other areas. Mentors can help them identify strengths and build the assets that are missing in their lives.

- **Relationships are key.** Strong relationships between adults and young people, between young people and their peers, and between teenagers and children are central to building assets. As a mentor, you have a significant opportunity to make a difference in your mentee's life, just by being there for him.

- **Asset building is an ongoing process.** It starts when a child is born and continues through high school and beyond. It's never too late to start building assets with and for your mentee, regardless of her age or what her life has been like up until now.

- **Consistent messages are important.** It is important for families, schools, communities, and others to give young people consistent and similar messages about what is important and what is expected of them. Mentors can play a critical role in exposing young people to positive messages, values, and examples; these messages can be modeled in action by the way you live your life and the way you and your mentee interact with each other and the world around you.

- **Intentional repetition is important.** Assets must be continually reinforced across the years and in all areas of a young person's life. As a significant adult in your mentee's life, you have a great opportunity to continually reinforce the positive messages and experiences he needs throughout his young life—and beyond.

CONTINUES →

When adults make deliberate efforts to help young people increase the number and degree of Developmental Assets they experience in their lives, it is called *asset building*. If you focus your energy on finding ways to help your mentee build these commonsense "assets" through your relationship, you stand a good chance of making a difference in her or his life.

SOME BASIC TIPS FOR HOW MENTORS CAN BUILD DEVELOPMENTAL ASSETS

- **Remember that the focus of mentoring is on forming a relationship and being a positive adult role model.** What you do during your regular visits with your mentee matters less than the fact that you are spending time together and providing your mentee with support and care.

- **Show your mentee that she is a priority by keeping in touch on a regular basis.** Even if you cannot be together very often, write letters, send cards, talk on the phone, or send e-mail or text messages.

- **Let your mentee know that you care about things that are important to him.** For example, if your mentee has a special friend or pet, ask regularly about how he is doing. If your mentee plays a sport, attend a game or match. If he sings or plays an instrument, ask for a personal recital once in a while.

- **Be flexible.** If your mentee has ideas about things to do or ways to do them, let her take the lead. You don't need a careful plan to build assets.

- **Get to know your mentee's interests and hobbies.** Help him find opportunities to get involved with organized activities or programs that use or develop those interests or hobbies.

- **Talk about and model your personal values.** Encourage your mentee to think about the values that are important to her and how those values affect behavior and decisions.

- **Share a new experience together,** such as fishing, visiting a local museum (some have days when entrance fees are waived or reduced), taking a class, eating at a new restaurant, or flying a kite.

- **Practice life skills together.** For example, prepare a meal together and serve it to your mentee's family or friends.

- **Emphasize the importance of a lifelong commitment to learning.** Go to the library together and check out books to read together. Help your mentee with homework or find someone who can.

- **Talk about some of your hopes and plans for the future and ask about your mentee's vision of the future.** Share ideas with each other about how you can make your respective dreams come true. If it seems as if your dreams can't or won't come true, work together to come up with ways to deal with barriers.

- **Enjoy your time together and have fun!**

12

The Role of Peer Mentors

CONGRATULATIONS!

It's great that you've decided to make a difference in the life of another young person by becoming a mentor. Hopefully you are excited about your new relationship, but you may also have some questions or worries.

As a young person, you may find that your role is slightly different from that of an adult mentor. Like any other mentor, you are a friend, a role model, and a listener. Here are some special things you might want to think about or discuss with program leaders when you are becoming a peer mentor:

When you think of yourself, your friends, or your classmates as a whole, what types of challenges do you see young people having?	**What kind of help do you think young people often need?**
How do peers hurt, rather than help, one another, sometimes making life even more difficult?	**What kinds of issues or problems are appropriate for a peer mentor to deal with? What kinds of situations might be better handled by an adult?**

13

Developmental Stages of Young People

You may feel as if it wasn't all that long ago that you yourself were taking that roller-coaster ride through adolescence. If you're a peer mentor, you still may be going through adolescence yourself. Or maybe you're an adult with children who have gone through or are currently going through adolescence. No matter what your level of experience is with young people, it helps to understand a little more about typical changes that happen to them as they approach and go through different stages. This helps you identify normal behaviors in your mentee and better equips you to react to them.

Below is a summary of typical developmental experiences of young people at different ages, as well as some tips for helping your mentee thrive during these critical developmental changes.

APPEARANCES AND SELF-IMAGE

By the time young people are between the ages of 10 and 12, they are well into puberty. As they age, they may worry about personal traits that are vital to them, but are hardly noticeable to others.

Young people also go through emotional changes that impact their self-image. By the time they are between the ages of 13 and 16, they will likely experience emotional extremes, from being happy to feeling sad or from thinking they are smart to believing they are dumb. They may want both to fit in with the crowd while at the same time stand out and be special. It is normal to see these kinds of emotional extremes continue well into their teen years as they take on more independence and make more decisions for themselves.

Tips for interacting with your mentee:

- Be sensitive to how she feels about her body or other issues.

- Acknowledge feelings, positive traits, and abilities, and help him recognize his own genuine worth.

- Make sure your mentee knows how important she is to you. Don't assume she knows.

- Bolster his self-confidence by emphasizing independent choice, encouraging self-respect, and recognizing positive behavior.

- Find out what your mentee loves learning about or what she's interested in studying.

DECISION MAKING FOR THE SHORT TERM AND THE FUTURE

Adolescents typically start to understand the consequences of different actions by about age 13 or 14. At this age they also are increasingly considering who they are in the world. As they age, adolescents mature in their ability to think through problems on their own. By the time young people are close to 17 or 18 years old, they are both excited and scared to be on their own.

Tips for interacting with your mentee:

- Encourage her to take responsibility for her actions.

- Help him make good choices, like getting his homework done before you do a fun activity together.

CONTINUES →

- Suggest that your mentee break planning and decision making down into a series of steps.

- Ask questions that highlight the positive results of good decisions and the unpleasant consequences of poor planning.

- Listen carefully without criticizing.

- Listen to your mentee's thoughts about the future.

- Support and respect his decisions.

- Offer ideas about what you think she might like to do or be good at.

- Find other mentors who can help direct his choices.

- Share your own excitement about the world and its possibilities.

RELATIONSHIPS WITH OTHERS

Generally, 10- to 12-year-olds still enjoy being around their family members. This is typically the age when romantic relationships start to become of interest, and friends and peers become even more important in their lives. As young people mature, they begin to actively seek out ways to be more independent of their family and to bond more closely with peers.

Tips for interacting with your mentee:

- At this age, young people are beginning to think like adults, but they don't have the experience and judgment needed to *act* like adults. Help your mentee recognize this.

- Suggest constructive behaviors, but provide multiple options to allow your mentee to make choices. For example, describe the positive aspects of helping a younger child with homework, doing chores without being asked, or volunteering with a friend at a local charity.

- Never give up on your mentee, even when things get tough.

14

Safety, Liability, and Boundaries

Every mentoring program has its own set of policies concerning issues of safety, liability, and appropriate boundaries between you, your mentee, and your mentee's family. Work with your program provider to complete this worksheet so that you can have all your program's safety policies "at a glance."

SAFETY, LIABILITY, OR BEHAVIOR ISSUE	OUR PROGRAM'S POLICY IS . . .
Where my mentee and I can (and cannot) meet	
How often I should meet with my mentee	
Spending time alone with my mentee	
Exchanging phone numbers	

CONTINUES →

SAFETY, LIABILITY, OR BEHAVIOR ISSUE	OUR PROGRAM'S POLICY IS . . .
Physical displays of affection (e.g., hugs)	
Contact with my mentee's family	
Mentee overnight visits at my home	
Transportation issues	
Mentee reports serious physical or emotional health issues (e.g. abuse or thoughts of suicide)	

15

Making the Time: Including Your Mentee in Your Already Busy Life

Some days it just seems impossible to wedge one more activity into your schedule. But being a mentor doesn't necessarily need to become a burden in your life. Being a mentor is about more than going on special outings to movies and amusement parks. It's about spending time together and being part of each other's lives.

For some mentees, joining you in your everyday activities may not be so "everyday" for them—these activities may be a rare exposure to a different kind of lifestyle or provide interesting opportunities to learn new skills. You can still designate special time for fun activities that you and your mentee enjoy together. But if your schedule or budget is tight at the moment, spending time together while completing daily tasks can help you avoid canceling your meetings or making your mentee feel you do not have time for her or him.

Try including your mentee in the following kinds of ordinary activities:

- **Preparing a meal.** You and your mentee can learn more about cooking, home budgeting, and etiquette by working together to select the menu, shop, prepare the meal, and, of course, enjoy the fruits of your labor!

- **Planning an event.** Are you hosting your next book club or having relatives over for a birthday party? Your mentee can learn event-planning skills by helping you with invitations, food and beverage preparations, room arrangement and decoration, and hosting the event.

- **Exercising.** Modeling healthy physical activity is a great way to teach your mentee the importance of exercise. Jog together at a local park or seek guest passes if you belong to a gym.

- **Projects around the house.** Does your faucet leak? Is your computer acting up again? Your mentee can acquire valuable vocational or household maintenance skills by learning with you about options for fixing the problem and joining you in repairing it. For some of these more mundane everyday tasks, you may want to have a bite to eat or play a board game so that the mentee feels some "fun" was thrown into the mix.

- **Family events.** Are you going to be attending a family gathering? Invite your mentee to join you.

- **Volunteering.** Do you donate your time to a local organization? Take your mentee along and help find meaningful ways he or she can contribute.

Of course, this principle works both ways. Here are a few ways you can join your mentee in activities that she has going on in her busy life:

- **Sporting events or other activities.** If your mentee is not already involved in some kind of organized activities, encourage her to join and take her to the practices. One mentor helped his mentee join a local chorus, and taking him to rehearsals became one of the activities they did together. Another match found an arena where both an adult and kids' hockey league were practicing at the same time.

- **Homework.** Help your mentee with his homework, or hang out and read a book while he finishes up.

- **Socializing.** Ask if you can join your mentee and a few of her friends for pizza.

CONTINUES →

Some mentoring programs have reasons to restrict your interactions with your mentee and limit you to a designated meeting place, such as a school or a residential setting for young people. Make sure you are familiar with your mentoring program's policies. If you are part of a program that allows you to choose your activity and location, you have the opportunity to think outside the box about when and where you and your mentee get together.

16

Mentors Aren't Made of Money

The temptation is common, and your intentions are good. Your relationship with your mentee is new. You want to give him the opportunity to experience things he may not get to do very often, if at all. There are so many possibilities—amusement parks, zoos, museums, movies, plays, concerts, professional sporting events—all a lot of fun, all providing an opportunity to strengthen your mentoring relationship, but all likely to require real money.

There is nothing wrong with wanting to help your mentee have many of the kinds of experiences she may not otherwise get. It is important, however, that these special outings are balanced with simpler, lower-cost activities, not just to save on the impact on your pocketbook, but also to ensure that you are not setting a precedent with your mentee that your relationship is based solely on participating in expensive outings.

You may want to start gathering ideas for ways to create meaningful interactions with your mentee that don't necessarily cost a lot of money, so you can be assured that the relationship is based on the important stuff—like support and caring—rather than on the places you go and the things you buy. You can ask your program staff for additional information about low-cost and no-cost activity ideas.

IDEAS FOR BALANCING ACTIVITIES THAT COST MONEY WITH LOW- OR NO-COST ACTIVITIES

- **For your first three to five meetings with your mentee, consider engaging only in low-cost or no-cost activities.** This can help set the precedent that not every visit will entail paying an admission fee or buying an expensive meal.

- **Consider making higher-cost activities (such as movies, sporting events, or concerts)** a celebration rather than an expectation. Perhaps the next time your mentee masters a song on the piano or improves a math grade on her next report card can be cause for a special celebration that involves a more expensive outing.

- **When taking your mentee to an event or activity that is more expensive, let him know how much "discretionary" money is available to spend on treats or souvenirs.** For example, before you get to the theater, let your mentee know that you only have $7 available for treats. You can help him make choices to stay within that amount, reminding him how much he has left. This not only helps set boundaries on spending, it also teaches invaluable budgeting skills!

- **Talk openly about how you place "value" on things in your life, and how that relates to spending money.** Maybe you prefer handmade gifts to ones bought in a store. Explain why those gifts make you happy. Perhaps you are saving your money to buy a new car. Explain the importance of forgoing less necessary expenses in your life such as pricey clothes or meals out in order to purchase a larger-ticket item.

- **Start a "savings account."** Even if you are just putting a few dollars in a simple envelope, set aside a limited amount of money each month. Ask your mentee to help manage the money and make decisions about spending it together.

- **Prioritize with your mentee what activities she would like to do with you in the future.** Your mentee may identify a range of activities with a range of costs attached to them. Map out as a team how you can intersperse lower-cost activities with higher-cost ones.

17

Engaging in Good Conversation

Conversations are the foundation of strong relationships, and strong relationships are the goal of meaningful mentoring. Engaging in the art of conversation does not always come naturally to people, and for many adolescents it can be a territory in which they have yet to build skills. (Ever have this conversation with a teen? "How are you doing?" "Fine." "How's school?" "Fine.")

Below are some tips for making conversations work, as well as some conversation starters to spark interesting discussions. Hopefully, they not only give you and your mentee something else to chat about once in a while, but also give you a chance to get to know each other a little better.

Tips for Making Conversations Work

- **Keep it going.** It's one thing to ask a question and then sit back to wait for an answer. It is another thing to really engage in a conversation. Asking follow-up questions or providing open-ended responses are great ways to keep the conversation going. The idea is not to debate an answer but to learn more. Try some of these:

  "That's cool. Tell me more."

  "You've really thought about this, haven't you?"

  "Are you saying . . . ?"

  "Interesting. Have you thought about . . . ?"

- **Conversation doesn't have to be "heavy."** It is important to have conversations about subjects that matter deeply, such as who are the most influential people in a young person's life. It is also important to listen to why a young person likes a certain fad, music star, or TV program. All conversations are meaningful when two people are truly engaged and interested in one another's questions and answers.

- **Be prepared for the unexpected answer.** You may ask a question and get an answer you did not want or expect. If an answer bothers you, simply listen and ask more questions about why the young person thinks and feels that way. Suspend your own judgment and let young people express their ideas and opinions.

- **Listening is most important.** Conversations with kids are better when we "elders" practice the art of listening. Through careful listening we tell them we care about their thoughts— and we care about them.

- **Timing can be everything.** If you ask a question that is met with silence or "the look," maybe this isn't the best time for a conversation. Or it could be that the specific question triggers a bigger issue for him, or he needs some time to process it. Taking a rain check on a question is okay.

- **Be prepared to give your own answer.** You are focusing on the young person, but she may also want to turn the question in your direction. This is a great chance to model thoughtful, honest responses.

18

Little Things Can Mean a Lot!

Mentors want to make a difference in the lives of their mentees, but how does that happen? Sometimes good things happen simply by how you two interact while spending time together. Having fun, getting to know each other, and just being together are all important ways to be there for your mentee.

Look for opportunities to make a bigger impact with the fun things you are already doing together. Use the chart below to identify ways to make those activities even more meaningful. Use the blank table on the next page to fill in ideas of your own.

Taking Our Activities to the Next Level

ACTIVITY	WHY IT'S GOOD FOR MY MENTEE	WHILE WE'RE AT IT . . .
Baking cookies	Baking is a good skill to learn; the conversations we have strengthen our relationship; and when we're done, we have cookies to eat!	I can encourage my mentee to take the lead in reading the recipe and measuring ingredients. When we're done, we could take cookies to a neighbor whose husband is ill.
Planting a garden	It's a satisfying activity when the plants start growing; they create a visual reminder of fun times together; and we have an opportunity for conversations about "harder" topics, since we don't necessarily have to be face-to-face.	We could take flowers we grew to someone who is feeling ill or down, or to thank someone for being there for us. We could plant and maintain a flower bed for someone with physical limitations.
Swapping books and magazines	It's fun; it helps us appreciate reading for pleasure; we can learn about each other's favorite reading materials.	We could choose books that address important social or emotional issues and read chapters aloud together.
Attending a professional baseball game	It's fun; it's exciting, especially if a home run ball comes your way; and we get to watch some of our favorite players.	I could start a conversation about players who have "made good" with their fame and fortune by supporting causes and valuing their family. We could talk about the reality of just how many athletes become professional. We could discuss other ways to make sports a part of your life besides being a professional athlete.

CONTINUES →

ACTIVITY	WHY IT'S GOOD FOR MY MENTEE	WHILE WE'RE AT IT . . .

19

Modeling Positive Behavior

Many would contend that, whether or not you are officially a "mentor," you are a role model in the lives of young people whom you encounter, just by the way you acknowledge them (or don't), show support and caring for others (or don't), and prioritize what really matters in your life. The question then really is, what *kind* of role model are you going to be? Since you have chosen to be a mentor, we can assume the answer to that question is that you want to be the best role model you can be.

Modeling admirable behavior does not mean you have to be a perfect human being who never makes mistakes and is a superhero in the eyes of your mentee. Instead, it means being intentional about letting your mentee see your positive behaviors toward others and the values you hold that drive you to behave the way you do. How do you treat the person taking your order at a fast-food restaurant? Why do you treat the person the way you do? How do you react when you have made a mistake that may have a negative effect on others (and may affect the way others perceive you as well)? As you already know, a lecture on how to be a good person probably isn't an effective strategy for teaching positive behavior. Little and big encounters during your time together will all be teachable moments where your mentee has the opportunity to see proper behavior in action.

Below are a few ideas for ways you can model being a caring, healthy, responsible adult. At the end of each list is a blank space where you can add an idea of your own.

MODELING SUPPORT

- Take turns telling each other about a family member who made a difference in your life and why. Make thank-you cards together so you can each thank that person for making a difference.

- If your program staff thinks it is appropriate, invite your mentee to visit your neighborhood. Introduce your mentee to the caring people who live there, or discuss ways you'd like to make your neighborhood a more positive environment.

- If your mentee is allowed to spend time around your family, engage in a healthy, supportive conversation with a family member in the presence of your mentee.

- *Your idea:*

MODELING EMPOWERMENT

- Take your mentee to a location where youth are given useful roles. For example, visit a park where teens are coaching younger children in sports.

- Invite your mentee to join you as you do volunteer work for a community organization.

- Ask your mentee to help you type up a list of emergency contact numbers. Talk about how the fire department or a poison control center can help people feel safe.

- *Your idea:*

CONTINUES →

MODELING BOUNDARIES AND EXPECTATIONS

- Talk about rules you had in your family growing up and what may have been good and bad about them. If you have children, talk about boundaries and expectations you have for them and why.

- Ask your mentee for advice on how you can support a friend or family member who is going through a rough time.

- Always refer to your mentee's future in terms of the possibilities and goals she can achieve, not in terms of limits or obstacles she needs to overcome.

- *Your idea:*

MODELING CONSTRUCTIVE USE OF TIME

- Invite your mentee to join you in a variety of activities, like creating artwork, listening to different types of music, or running in a race for charity.

- Challenge each other to spend less time in front of "screens" (TV, video games, computers) during your free time. Make it a friendly competition.

- Schedule your time together to include a balance of learning, working, talking, and fun activities.

- *Your idea:*

MODELING COMMITMENT TO LEARNING

- Share with your mentee all the ways you continue to learn, whether it's by showing him how you have been putting together a family tree or by demonstrating a new technique you've learned to improve your backstroke.

- Read for pleasure. Start a book club with your mentee, and perhaps invite others to join you.

- *Your idea:*

MODELING POSITIVE VALUES

- Demonstrate the "Golden Rule" in action—whether ordering from a server at a restaurant or saying hello to young people in the mall, treat others the way you want to be treated.

- Admit when you are wrong. Apologize sincerely and talk about what you learned from the experience.

- Invite your mentee to get involved with you in causes that matter to both of you.

- *Your idea:*

MODELING SOCIAL COMPETENCIES

- Invite your mentee to attend events in places where people of different cultural/racial/ethnic backgrounds are a majority.

- When one of you loses your temper, step back and talk about other ways that your frustration could have been communicated.

- *Your idea:*

MODELING POSITIVE IDENTITY

- When talking about someone, emphasize the strengths that person has.

- Help your mentee learn about college options. Work on applications together or visit campuses if possible.

- Does your mentee have career ideas? Jointly look into them. Find people already engaged in those careers to learn what it takes to be successful.

- *Your idea:*

20

Common Phases of a Mentoring Relationship

Every relationship—friendships, parent–child, sibling, marriage—goes through different stages or cycles as it matures. At each stage, mentors and mentees may experience some common anxieties and behaviors that reflect what is happening in the relationship at that stage.

The Big Brothers Big Sisters program of the Greater Twin Cities in Minneapolis, Minnesota, outlines four stages in the growth cycle of a mentoring match, as well as some helpful strategies for successfully navigating each stage:

❶ Beginning the relationship—In this stage mentors and mentees are testing the waters with each other. Mentees may feel nervous or wary, and they may be putting on their best behavior for you. They may also get frustrated if things don't go as they expected. You as a mentor may want to "fix" everything. You may find yourself adjusting your initial expectations about being a mentor, once you've experienced it for real. Both of you may be trying to bridge each other's age, cultural, and lifestyle differences as well as finding things in common.

Strategies for this stage:

- Be consistent and reliable.

- Show you are willing to listen.

- Focus on doing things *with* rather than *for* your mentee.

- Be aware of your own feelings about age, cultural, and lifestyle differences.

- Be nonjudgmental.

- Reach out, be available.

- Be open and honest about what you can, can't, or have to do.

❷ Building trust—Now that the two of you know each other better and have some shared experiences under your belt, you and your mentee may experience greater trust. Your mentee may be coming out of his shell, feeling better about himself, or simply more confident because you have demonstrated that you care. As a result, he may share more information with you. He may start to rely on you more for support and validation in this stage, possibly to the point of becoming overdependent. At this stage, you may be experiencing more satisfaction with the mentoring relationship. You also may, however, be feeling overwhelmed by the extent of the issues faced by the mentee.

Strategies for this stage:

- Be patient.

- Expect setbacks.

- If you think your mentee is becoming too dependent, set limits around the frequency and duration of visits and encourage him to broaden his support network.

- Be involved, yet keep perspective.

- Continue to be consistent and reliable.

- Continue to treat your mentee as capable.

CONTINUES →

3 **Testing the relationship**—Now that rapport and trust are built, it is typical for the mentee to start testing boundaries in the relationship. Deep down, she may still want to see just how much staying power this relationship really has. Your mentee may make inappropriate requests of you. She may even show resentment or hostility toward you. You may start resenting what seems like negative behavior, and you might also feel caught in the middle between your mentee, her family, or other service providers.

Strategies for this stage:

- Don't take testing personally.
- Reinforce limits, if necessary.
- Continue to treat your mentee as capable.
- Reaffirm your intention to remain in the relationship.

4 **Increasing independence**—Once you have come through the trust building and relationship testing, you may find your mentee becoming less dependent on you and finding other sources of support. On the upside, you might see an increased self-worth in your mentee. However, setbacks are still possible during this stage as your mentee may take bigger risks in his life and in the relationship. As a result of all of this, you may feel discouraged or less needed during this stage.

Strategies for this stage:

- Point out the shifts in behavior that you are observing and reinforce your mentee's efforts to seek support from others.
- Continue to support your mentee while encouraging independence.
- Expect some setbacks as a natural part of this stage.

21

Are We Having Fun Yet?!

This isn't how you pictured your relationship with your mentee turning out. She was supposed to burst out the door of her home with excitement every time you picked her up, hang on your every word, and spend at least half of her time with you laughing and smiling. Hasn't quite worked out that way? There can be any number of reasons why your mentee doesn't appear to find your time together as enjoyable as you hoped. Some of those reasons may have nothing to do with you.

One mentor had been taking her mentee to a wide variety of restaurants, in the hope he would learn about foods he had never tried. She was sure he would be especially excited at a Mongolian barbecue, where he could assemble his own ingredients and watch a cook stir-fry them. Instead, he was not very responsive, and she was discouraged that he seemed unimpressed. However, when she met his parents two months later, they said he had raved about the restaurant and convinced the family to go there! This mentor learned that she couldn't necessarily judge the impact of her efforts by her mentee's outward reactions.

There are several things you can try that can get below the surface to identify what your mentee is really feeling.

- **Be patient.** Dig a little deeper to see what the real issue is. It could just be that trust is still being built between you and your mentee, and she is just testing you to see if you will leave (possibly like others in her life have before you). Young people don't respond well to pressure, especially young people in need of a positive adult role model. Find avenues that are natural outlets for your mentee to talk, and eventually she may share what is blocking her from enjoying her time with you.

- **Identify activities jointly.** Research shows that empowering the mentee to select activities you'll do during your visits together is one of the factors that contributes to the success of a mentor–mentee relationship. One mentor–mentee match had two jars, one filled with low-cost activities the mentor wanted to do, the other with low-cost ideas the mentee wanted to do. They took turns picking an activity from their jar during each visit.

- **Ask a family member for ideas.** Parents and caregivers like to be asked their opinions. If your program allows you to be in contact with your mentee's family, consider talking on the phone or meeting for coffee to gain some ideas or insights. Check this out with your mentee first to be sure he feels comfortable with this effort.

- **Help her past her shyness.** It could be that your mentee is just shy and having a hard time opening up. One mentee was a very quiet child. After several visits, her mentor told her she would tell her whole life story to the mentee and keep talking until the mentee "cried uncle." It got both of them laughing and broke the ice a little.

22

Motivating Your Mentee to Want to Learn

One of the most important contributions mentors can make in the lives of mentees is exposing them to new ideas and instilling in them a love of learning. Learning, of course, happens in school, and building academic skills and relevance is very important. However, discovery obviously also happens out in the world—studying other places, learning how to do fun activities or hobbies, finding out about potential careers.

Below are some tips for helping mentees embrace learning as something they want to do because it is fun and relevant, not just because they "have to" learn to get by in school.

- **Make it fun.** This may be obvious, but the more learning is tied to the interests of your mentee, the easier it is to promote learning. If what you're trying is losing steam, change course and try another strategy.

- **Work on it.** One mentor bought an inexpensive math workbook for her mentee, and they spent 10–20 minutes per visit doing worksheets. The mentor gave a lot of verbal praise and checked over her mentee's work. When she completed the book, they bought a second workbook for the next grade level.

- **Trust that learning is natural.** Look for alternative ways to help a mentee learn something. Some kids learn differently from ways that are taught in traditional school

settings. Your mentee may get more excited about studying plant life walking through a park instead of reading a textbook.

- **Acknowledge the mentee's doubts that learning can be fun.** One staff person at a mentoring program noted that she had seen young people avoid learning opportunities as a way to get attention. Give your mentee the attention she seeks, but then ask her to help brainstorm ideas for making learning more fun.

- **Show how school applies to life.** This is especially important for older mentees. Take him on college tours. Arrange for informational interviews with professionals in your mentee's area of interest. If your mentee likes fashion, explain how math is used in designing clothing and how marketing experts use psychology and human behavior information to create ads. If your mentee likes fixing things, talk about how physics, electricity, or other sciences are involved.

Simple Ideas Mentors Have Used to Make Learning Enjoyable

- Learn about another country, and cook a traditional meal from each other's culture.

- Read a book together.

- Do hands-on projects (such as woodworking, crafts, or gardening).

23

Family Relationships

Adolescence is a time when young people naturally begin to exert their independence from their families. It is also a time of more volatile emotions. All of this alone can naturally cause stress on the home front for teens and their parents or caregivers and siblings. Add to this mix any other stresses on a family—such as divorce, financial problems, health issues, or legal challenges—and an adolescent's already stressful existence can be thrown into overdrive.

Rest assured that just by being a constant, positive presence in your mentee's life, you can help her or him through the ups and downs of life. But there are times when, as a caring nonfamily adult in your mentee's life, you may need to provide extra support. So how can you help your mentee through changing family relationships and challenges without crossing the line into interfering? This is a tough distinction, and you can always consult program staff for assistance with difficult situations. Here are some additional ideas for helping your mentee with family interactions:

- **Let your mentee know you are there for her, no matter what.** Be a constant source of support even when her family is struggling.

- **Point out the positive things that are happening in his family.** When a family member shows love or caring, be sure your mentee notices.

- **Assure your mentee that she is a good person with gifts and talents to contribute.** Tell her about specific times when you have observed her being a good daughter, sibling, grandchild, or friend.

- **When conflict arises, help your mentee separate the person he is in conflict with from that person's behavior.** Mom may be a fun, caring person who made a big mistake.

Help your mentee focus his frustration with family members on behaviors, not on the persons themselves.

- **Talk about why families enforce boundaries on young people.** A curfew that seems unfair may be in place because parents and caregivers want to protect their child.

- **Continue to have high expectations for your mentee's behavior and achievement.** Don't allow family situations to be used as a barrier or an excuse.

- **Help your mentee strategize the many ways she could confront a difficult family situation,** weighing the pros and cons of each approach.

- **Advocate for your mentee's health and safety.** It is possible that your mentee's parent or caregiver is not making good choices on your mentee's behalf. If you suspect that his home situation is in serious turmoil that could escalate to abuse or neglect, talk to program staff about your concerns. Ask them to connect the family to professional services. Do not try to step in and mediate the situation yourself.

- **Reach out to your mentee's family early on in the relationship to help build strong support for the mentoring relationship.** Be sure to honor any policies the mentoring program has in place regarding whether or how you can interact with your mentee's caregivers. If the program encourages mentor interaction with parents, and you are comfortable doing so, find ways to build rapport and trust with them. It may take months before a parent or caregiver is comfortable reaching out to you, but eventually you and your mentee's family may be able to build a strong alliance of support for your mentee.

24

Keeping Things Fresh

When you spend enough time with someone, inevitably your relationship reaches a point where the newness feels as if it has worn off. Maybe at one point your mentee was full of surprises, revealing a little more of his true self at every visit. Now you generally know what to expect from him, you know a lot about what is going on in his life, and you've tried out a lot of the fun activities you planned to do when you were first matched with your mentee.

There is something comfortable about reaching this "familiar" point in a relationship, but you run the risk of one (or both) of you losing your enthusiasm. As with any good relationship, highs and lows are normal; it takes conscious effort to keep a relationship going and growing. How can you keep things fun and fresh in your relationship so that you and your mentee don't get bored with it?

Here are some tips for maintaining relationship energy:

- **Have a heart-to-heart talk about the ups and downs in every relationship, and stress that they are natural.** The key is to understand it and intentionally find ways to avoid a downward spiral from which it could be difficult to rebound.

- **Brainstorm new activities to do together.** One mentor–mentee match decided that at every visit they would take turns picking something totally spontaneous to do, and there could be no griping or whining about it. On one visit the mentor chose an unlikely activity—

going to the opera. It turns out the mentee, a teen from a rough urban neighborhood, loved the experience; eventually he bought the soundtrack and played it in his mentor's car.

- **Set goals for your relationship.** Make a timeline for all the activities you'll do over the next year. Throw in some really outrageous activities as well as some of your standard, tried-and-true activities. If you live in a rural area, consider an activity that gets you to a bigger city, or vice versa. Remember that fun activities can be very low-cost.

- **Empowering your mentee to share her thoughts and feelings is crucial.** A natural pitfall mentors fall into is that they feel obligated to impart wisdom or advice to a child. Often, what the child needs most is to have you listen to him and empower him to solve his own problems. Giving your mentee a chance to talk and work through problems on her own will keep her engaged in the relationship.

- **Be sensitive to the developmental stage your mentee is in, and find out about other stresses in his life.** Don't just presume you know what is going on in your mentee's life. Today's young people are often dealing with a different set of issues than you may have dealt with in your youth. Things may be happening in your mentee's life that are impacting how he responds to your relationship. Let him know you are there to support him, no matter what.

Seeking Additional Support

The mentoring program you participate in likely has policies and procedures in place for seeking professional support when mentees need it (or mentors suspect they need it). Always go to your program's staff first for support, and do not hesitate to do so at any time.

Your role as a mentor is that of a friend, confidant, advocate, and role model. However, if you are concerned that your mentee either has or may have challenges in her life that feel beyond your expertise (perhaps she has a learning disability, or you suspect she is experimenting with drugs), seeking information can be helpful for you to more fully understand what is going on in your mentee's life, and can give you important insight into how to more effectively support her. For example, finding out about a mentee's learning disability can help you identify effective ways to help her with her homework.

It is important to remember, in the midst of learning more about your mentee's challenges and helping support him through it, that you are still a mentor. You should advocate for his health and safety, and support him to get on a healthier path, but if you suspect your mentee is in danger of being harmed or neglected by whatever challenge he is facing, or if you suspect he is breaking the law, you need to report the issue to the mentoring program's staff.

Here are some tips for how to support a mentee who is experiencing a challenge in her or his life:

- **Make sure you know your mentoring program's policies and procedures** for dealing with these types of challenges.

- **Make sure you know about any legal standards for mandatory reporting** dictated by your state or province.

- **Let your mentee know up front that you want to be there for her anytime she needs someone to talk to and that you are her advocate.** Part of being an advocate is getting help when you suspect she is involved in a dangerous or unhealthy situation. If your mentee tells you about something in her life that requires professional attention, you are obliged, as her advocate, to report the situation so that she can get help. The downside to this approach is that you run the risk of your mentee shutting you out from what is going on in her life for fear of getting in trouble. But your mentee needs to know not only that you want to be there for her because you care, but also that you are *obligated* to be supportive of her, which may mean finding help for her from outside the relationship.

- **Allow your mentoring program staff to communicate with families directly or to contact professional services your mentee may need.** They are the neutral outside party in the situation that can more safely make these contacts without putting you in a position to do so as a volunteer.

- **Find out more about what your mentee is going through and how it may be affecting him.** If you suspect abuse or neglect, contact program staff immediately. Try to learn more about the issue and how it may be shaping your mentee's interactions with others and his view of himself. Your purpose here is better understanding of what is going on in your mentee's life so that you can be more responsive to his needs, not to seek out solutions or ways you can "cure" his problems single-handedly.

26

Exploring Opportunities for Growth

All young people have gifts, talents, and potential. They may not know how to act on those strengths, or, for whatever reason, they may not choose to channel their strengths in productive ways. Perhaps they are insecure about their potential to achieve success, or perhaps their view of success is just too narrow, limited to people like professional athletes, musicians, actors, corporate CEOs, or doctors.

An important role mentors can play with mentees is to help them define success as making choices that open the doors to numerous options for their future, rather than choosing to engage in activities that can close doors.

When thinking about helping a young person see her or his potential for a brighter future, consider the ideas below for building assets.

EXTERNAL ASSETS

SUPPORT

- **Let your mentee know when you "catch" him doing something impressive.** Be specific about what actions you thought were impressive and how they could help him move forward. For example: "I am really impressed with how you made sure you had your homework done before we got together today. It shows me that learning is a priority for you, and that you have good time management skills. The people at my work who get the most respect are the ones that are always taking the initiative to learn and who can juggle their schedule to get a lot done."

EMPOWERMENT

- **Encourage your mentee to take the initiative to plan at least half of your outings,** including how you'll get there and what you'll do once you're there. Follow her lead.

- **Help your mentee channel his gifts and interests into a volunteer, job shadow, or internship experience.** If he enjoys surfing the Web, suggest that he volunteer at a senior center or library helping older people or young children learn how to get around on the Internet. Is she good at fixing bikes? Suggest that she work with her school to find an internship experience with a bike repair shop.

BOUNDARIES AND EXPECTATIONS

- **Help your mentee meet people who are in careers he is interested in pursuing.** Do some research together on what it takes to succeed in that field, and what someone realistically needs to do to enter that field. This can be a fine balance between encouraging your mentee to dream big and helping him be realistic. He may want to be a professional basketball player, so he should find out all he can about what paths pro ballplayers take to make it to the top (e.g. summer camps and college plays). At the same time, he needs to know up front that only a very small percentage of people who play basketball will become professionals. He needs to know that some people make it to the professional level, only to have their career ended at a very young age by an injury. What would happen then?

CONTINUES →

CONSTRUCTIVE USE OF TIME

▪ **Encourage your mentee to take activities she has always done to the next level.** Has she been a member of the Boys and Girls Club for a long time? Help her pursue leadership and volunteer activities within the club. Perhaps she has been active in her congregation's youth programs; maybe now is a good time to think about volunteering to teach or assist in a religious class for young children.

INTERNAL ASSETS

COMMITMENT TO LEARNING

▪ **Expose your mentee to other worlds through reading.** Start your own book club. Is he interested in learning more about Africa? Go to your library or on the Internet to find books about Africa; watch a movie that is set in Africa; and look up facts about a particular country's people, government, and cultures. Talk about ways your mentee could someday visit Africa, maybe through a study abroad program at a university, volunteering through the Peace Corps, or saving up for an African safari on his own or with friends. Investigate those possibilities; collect pictures and information in a notebook that the mentee can refer to often to keep his interest active.

POSITIVE VALUES

▪ Does your mentee have a passion for promoting equality and justice? **Help her think about ways she can channel that passion into action, both now and in the future.** This could be in the form of volunteering at a local organization that promotes these issues, joining an online community that supports the rights of others, or pursuing career options for promoting justice, from social work and advocacy to law and politics.

▪ **Talk about ethics in the workplace.** When news headlines talk about executives who stole funds from their companies or a politician who accepted a bribe, use it as an opportunity to engage your mentee in a discussion about right and wrong in the workplace.

SOCIAL COMPETENCIES

▪ If your mentee is considering getting a job, **help her build skills such as answering interview questions and writing a résumé.** If you don't feel confident about your own skills in this area, try finding a related community education class to take together.

▪ **Talk about instances when you have encountered conflict or other difficult situations** in your own life. How did you handle them? In hindsight, what would you have done differently?

POSITIVE IDENTITY

▪ **See your mentee as a whole person.** Always view your mentee as a person with possibilities. Avoid focusing only on the obstacles in his life.

▪ **Help your mentee find her sense of purpose in life.** Connect her gifts, talents, and interests with potential ways she can use them to launch a career, have a happy family, or change the world.

27

What to Do When the Relationship Ends

It is important to remember that every mentoring relationship will end at some point, whether your mentee simply outgrows the relationship as she moves toward adulthood or one of you decides to end the relationship before that. It is normal for many kinds of relationships in our lives to end, and mentoring relationships are often designed to only last for a specific amount of time. No matter what circumstances have led to the end of your formal mentoring relationship, you have a responsibility to do what you can to make the conclusion as smooth as possible. It is possible that you will find it difficult or painful when the time comes, but below are some ideas for weathering the transition with grace and integrity.

IN GENERAL

- **Avoid the blame game.** It doesn't matter which one of you initiates the end of the relationship. Remember that most friendships change over time, and sometimes they simply end in healthy ways. The important thing is to strive for a considerate parting rather than a sudden or hurtful loss.

- **Offer to continue to be in your mentee's life in some capacity.** You may not see each other as often, but offer to write letters, visit him, and be present at future milestones (a recital, game, graduation ceremony), leaving it up to the mentee to decide if he would want that. Don't make promises you can't keep.

- **Talk about what you found most important and satisfying about your relationship** with your mentee, and encourage her to do the same. Even if your relationship has been rocky,

there is always something positive in the time mentors and mentees spend together.

- **Talk about how you feel about the change,** and encourage your mentee to do the same.

- Sit down with your mentee and **write down all the things you did together** over the past year. It may conjure up some sadness, but you may also find yourself laughing at some of the fonder moments you've shared.

- **Let your mentee know how much she means to you.** Thank her for the opportunity to get to know her. Let her know how she has changed you for the better, and point out the improvements you have seen in her behavior, skills, or disposition.

- **If your program allows you to continue contact, try not to completely cut yourself off from your mentee after the formal relationship ends,** even if he seems to be shutting you out. Letters, e-mails, and calls to catch up with him and remind him how important he is to you will still register and help the situation.

IF YOU ARE THE ONE WHO NEEDS TO END THE RELATIONSHIP

- **Make sure you are very certain that ending the formal mentoring relationship is the only workable option.** Talk to your mentoring program staff about options to reduce the number of meetings or other ways you can work in visits.

- **Tell your mentee in person.** You might be more comfortable talking about this in the

CONTINUES →

presence of staff from the mentoring program. Be honest but careful. If lack of time is the issue, don't leave your mentee thinking he is not important to you. Rather, frame the conversation about the strengths your mentee has, the changes he has made in your life, and the realities you face (demanding job, household responsibilities) that are unavoidable.

- **Make sure your mentee's family knows about the change.** Either ask your mentoring program staff to tell the family or tell them yourself. This will help give them time to prepare ways they can support their child through the transition.

28

Looking Back on Your Mentoring Experience

You've experienced mentoring firsthand—the ups and downs, the small victories and the setbacks. You may spend a lot of your energy focusing on how this relationship has affected your mentee. But in order to make a healthy transition into a different stage, it is important for you, the mentor, to take stock in what *you* have gained from the mentoring experience and, just as important, what impact your mentee has had on you.

Below are some questions to help you reflect on your mentoring experience. If you feel comfortable, discuss this handout and share your answers with your mentee.

Taking Stock of My Mentoring Experience

What has mentoring taught me about myself?	
What has mentoring taught me about the world around me?	
Am I satisfied with how I have mentored my mentee?	
What three things am I proudest of?	

CONTINUES →

Do I have any regrets about the relationship or how I have handled it?	
When mentoring gets tough, what has kept me coming back to her/him?	
What are my mentee's strengths?	
What has he or she taught me?	
What will I always remember about being a mentor?	
In hindsight, was there anything that would have made being a mentor easier? (Note: You may want to share these thoughts with your mentoring program staff so that they can continue to improve how they support mentoring relationships.)	
Because of my mentoring experience, what will I do more, less, or differently in my life?	

MENTEES

Historically, our society has viewed the "client" of any social program as simply a passive recipient of an organization's services. For some mentoring programs, this means mentors and program staff unintentionally deliver help *to* mentees instead of working *with* young people. An asset-building approach goes beyond this concept to welcome mentees as active contributors to the mentoring team, treating them as important players in the success of a mentoring relationship and in their own development.

This next section will encourage mentees to make the most of their mentoring relationship as a way of taking their positive development to the next level. The handouts that follow provide another collection of helpful tools you can offer mentees as they meet their mentors and learn more about this type of friendship. Once again, the Developmental Assets framework adds structure and additional meaning to the advice.

You are not just in the business of matching young people with mentors. You are also helping build a foundation for mentees to grow into healthy, caring, and responsible adults. Empowering them to take charge of their own healthy development is an important way to make the mentoring relationship stronger and more meaningful.

29

My Mentor's Role in My Life

SO WHAT'S A MENTOR REALLY SUPPOSED TO DO?

Mentors are people who are older than you who like kids and want to spend time with a special younger person like you. Through your friendship with your mentor, you'll get a chance to try fun things, learn new skills, and have another person in your life that likes you just the way you are, a person you can turn to when you need support and comfort. Because every person is different, there is no one perfect way to be a mentor. But here are some basic things mentors are and are not.

YOUR MENTOR IS . . .

. . . a friend. Like any friendship, mentors and mentees do fun things together. They also teach each other, help each other, and are honest with each other. And sometimes they might want to have conversations about things that make them feel worried or upset.

. . . a role model. Mentors try to set a good example for how to live. Mentors are not perfect people. Your mentor will do his best to share with you what he's good at, and he should be honest about mistakes he has made or things he is not good at doing.

. . . a listener you can trust. You may say things to your mentor that you don't feel comfortable saying to anyone else. Sometimes you may tell your mentor about your hopes, dreams, or fears. Other times you may reveal mistakes you've made. Mentors have your best interests in mind and try to be supportive of you, regardless of what you confide in them.

. . . someone who is proud of you. Your mentor should be able to see all the talents you have and help you learn and grow. She can help you take actions that make a positive difference to others in your family, neighborhood, school, or community.

YOUR MENTOR IS NOT. . .

. . . a mentor to your family. His role is to provide special attention to you. While getting to know your family can help him understand you better, his energy and attention should be focused on you.

. . . a social worker or doctor. You may tell something to your mentor, or she may think something is going on in your life, and she may need to ask for help from other people in order to help you. This is because some problems you face may be complicated, and your mentor might need professional help in order to be the best mentor to you that she can be.

. . . a "fixer." Your mentor is not trying to change you or make you "better." Of course, his support can help you overcome hurdles in your life. But don't forget that you have gifts and talents; you have a lot to offer the world. Your mentor's job is to help you build and use those gifts and talents to make a difference in your life and the lives of others.

CONTINUES →

WHAT'S MY ROLE AS A MENTEE?

As a "mentee" (which means someone who has a mentor), you have a role to play in making a good relationship with your mentor, too.

REMEMBER TO...

. . . give your mentor a chance. Nobody's perfect, and it may not seem at first like you have much in common. But give it some time, and try to get to know her. You may be surprised at how much you can enjoy being with your mentor once you get to know her.

. . . show your mentor you appreciate him. Tell him when you've had fun with him. Thank him when he has spent time with or money on you. This will help your mentor feel good about the time you spend together.

. . . be open to new experiences. Your mentor may ask you to try new things. Maybe it's a different kind of food, or maybe it's a trip to a museum. Give it a chance.

. . . share what you know. Don't be afraid to share your talents and interests with your mentor. Maybe it's the words to your favorite song, or maybe it's advice on how to play tennis. You have important knowledge and skills to share.

30

Communicating with My Mentor

WHAT IF MY MENTOR WANTS TO TALK ABOUT THINGS THAT AREN'T EASY TO TALK ABOUT?

At some point in your relationship, your mentor may ask you questions about important stuff—how you're doing in school, what's going on with your family, or what you do when you're hanging out with your friends. Sometimes she might even bring up a topic that bothers you. Maybe she asked you about something that upsets you or makes you uncomfortable. Or maybe you're just not interested in talking about some things.

Here are some ideas to keep in mind as you learn to talk with your mentor:

➜ **Take things slowly.** Get to know each other before you start talking about really important things.

➜ **Be honest with her.** If you already know that talking about school just stresses you out, for example, tell your mentor. One mentee told his mentor the first time they met that he never wanted to talk about school. For nine years his mentor never brought up the subject of school. It worked great for them.

➜ **You don't have to share deeper conversations with your mentor until you feel good and comfortable.** There's nothing wrong with your mentor and you keeping your conversations and activities about fun things, even for a long time. After a while, you may trust her enough to talk about important issues and concerns in your life, but for some people it takes a long time to get to that point.

➜ **Test it out when you're ready to discuss deeper things.** Try talking about one thing that makes you a bit uncomfortable. Your mentor might be a great listener or have some helpful ideas. Start by saying, "I've been thinking about something, but I'm feeling a little shy about discussing it." This will help your mentor be respectful and kind while you are talking.

➜ **Be kind to your mentor.** Chances are your mentor doesn't mean to make you upset when he brings up tough issues. More likely, he's bringing them up because he cares about you. When you tell him you don't want to talk about something, try saying, "I'm glad you care about this, but I just don't want to talk about it."

31

What Are Developmental Assets?

Do you ever wonder: Who am I? Where do I fit it in? How do I figure out what's important to me? How can I reach my dreams?

If you're wondering about these things, you're not alone; they're questions most people want to figure out. How you answer these questions is part of what makes you unique—and can help you follow your dreams.

Trying to figure out the answers can be difficult and confusing, but there's a lot that can help you along the way. The choices you make and the way you live your life, including doing your best in school and staying healthy and safe, are strongly linked with having what researchers call Developmental Assets. Grouped into eight categories, the assets are positive qualities, skills, characteristics, and experiences that young people need. (If you haven't received a copy of the complete list, you can visit www.search-institute.org/assets/assetlists to learn more.) By focusing on assets, you can aim toward being your best—a person happy to be alive; someone who makes the most of every day with a positive attitude; a person others look up to, count on, trust, and respect.

Below is a list of the eight categories of assets that young people need in order to be caring, healthy, and responsible. There are also ideas for how you can build these assets in your own life.

♥ **Support**—All of us need to feel loved, cared for, appreciated, accepted, and included. Support is about being there for others, and others being there for you.

To get more support in your life, work on forming good relationships. For example:

→ When you don't know how to connect with someone new, try telling a little bit about yourself to get started. You could say, "I just heard the best song," and see where that goes.

→ Be respectful of what the other person prefers. Some people feel fine asking for help; others would rather you offered them help first.

✴ **Empowerment**—All of us need to feel that people believe we have something important to give the world and encourage us to contribute our time and talents. Empowerment is about feeling valuable.

To become more empowered, think about what you're willing to work on. For example:

→ When you're feeling powerless, look for opportunities to help other people in your community.

→ Pitch in with chores at home or volunteer to be on a safety committee at school. Find useful roles like these in all aspects of your life.

⭐ **Boundaries and Expectations**—We all need to know that what people expect of us is reasonable and also challenges us to do our best.

Sometimes adults need help seeing that you're ready to have more responsibility and freedom. Being patient and willing to negotiate and showing respect and responsibility will make discussions about what's in bounds and what's out of bounds go more smoothly.

CONTINUES →

→ Think about a time when you were proud of yourself because you tried hard. Remembering those times can help you keep having high expectations of yourself.

→ Talk openly with an adult about a rule you'd like to change. Think about ways to meet in the middle on a new version of the rule.

Constructive Use of Time—When you can make the most of your time by balancing what you *need* to do with what you *like* to do, you'll get more done, develop a stronger sense of purpose, and have more fun. For example:

→ One way to balance what you have to do with what you want to do is get chores or homework out of the way first; then you can enjoy your "down" time without feeling guilty or being nagged.

→ Try an activity you've never done before. Spend time in a club, on a team, or attending religious activities.

Commitment to Learning—There's not much chance of having the life you want without at least a high school education. If you make it a goal to work hard, even in subjects you don't like, you can reward yourself by spending more time learning about what you really like. You can find many ways to improve your learning. For example:

→ Think about what you like to learn and what you don't. For example, try classes taught by teachers you've heard other students really like, even if they're subjects you're not sure about. It may be easier to learn something when your teacher cares about you and is excited about what he or she is teaching.

→ Ask an adult to teach you a new skill, such as fishing or cooking. Remember that not all learning happens in a classroom.

Positive Values—Positive values encourage you to match what you do with what you believe. Acting regularly on your positive values gives you the confidence to make your own decisions without feeling as if you have to follow the crowd. It makes

you the leader of yourself (and maybe others, too).

To act on your positive values, show others what you care about. For example:

→ Choose a social problem, such as homelessness, to help work on. Try not to be discouraged by the size and difficulty of a problem—that just means your help is needed even more.

→ Ask another person, such as your mentor, to share her or his beliefs on a topic that interests you. This may give you new ideas about living out your own beliefs.

Social Competencies—Being a good friend, accepting differences in people, working through disagreements nonviolently, and planning ahead to avoid problems are all key skills that help you feel comfortable around others and good about yourself. This is what social competencies are all about. Think about these ideas:

→ You will get along with people better if you can learn to think about something for a while before acting and if you can consider how others might feel and respect them even if you disagree.

→ Plan an event with your mentor. Talk together about the steps you need to do to make it happen. When the event is done, think back on the planning. What went well? What would you do differently next time?

Positive Identity—When you have self-esteem, you have confidence in who you are and can talk comfortably and proudly about what makes you unique. When you believe in your ability to make good things happen, you feel more hopeful.

To develop a positive identity, pay attention to how you think about yourself and your future. For example:

→ Focus on your best skills and give yourself credit for the things you try but don't do so well.

→ Imagine and find out what you could do after high school that suits your interests and talents. What would it be like to be a wildlife photographer? A mechanic? A teacher?

32

Handling Conflict with My Mentor

WHAT DO I DO WHEN THERE'S A PROBLEM?

Hopefully you and your mentor will have plenty of meaningful conversations and fun adventures as you get to know each other. Whether you become friends slowly or get along right away, there may be a few times when you feel annoyed, frustrated, or even angry with your mentor. It's important to remember that *all* friendships go through tough times, and learning to get past them can make your friendships even stronger.

Sometimes conflicts can make you feel as if no solution is possible, and giving up is the only option. Try not to get discouraged. Your mentor cares about you and doesn't want a problem to get in the way of your friendship. So what do you do when you are having trouble? The chart below offers a few ideas you can try.

Talk about what you expect.	Before a problem happens, try to let your mentor know about things that matter to you or make you upset. Here are some examples: ➡ "I hope you'll always call me if you're going to miss a meeting." ➡ "Please don't ask me a lot of questions about my friends. I like to have my privacy." ➡ "I'm kind of a picky eater, so I hope you won't put a lot of pressure on me to eat things I don't like."
Learn that it's okay to disagree.	You and your mentor probably aren't going to agree on everything, and that's just fine. It doesn't mean anything is wrong. You're just two different people getting to know each other, and it's okay to have different opinions.
Use "I" statements.	You might feel like saying, "You make me so mad," or "You never call me." Instead, try starting your sentences with "I" and describe your own feelings without blaming your mentor. Here are some examples: ➡ "I feel sad when our meetings are canceled because it makes me feel as if our friendship doesn't get enough attention." ➡ "I feel embarrassed when you ask me about girlfriends because I'm not really interested in dating."

CONTINUES →

Listen respectfully.	Even when you feel upset, try to remember that your mentor has feelings, too. Give your mentor a chance to talk about the conflict. Pay close attention and try not to interrupt. When your mentor has finished speaking, ask questions to make sure you understand how he or she feels. Here are some questions you might use: → "I'm not sure I understand what you mean. Will you please say more about it?" → "Can you give me some examples to help me understand better?" → "Have you had a conflict like this before? What did you do to solve that problem?"
Talk to another caring adult.	Sometimes you might not feel ready to talk with your mentor about a problem. Instead, you might find it helpful to talk with an adult in your family or with a staff person at the mentoring program. Other adults can help you sort out your feelings and think of ways to make the problem better. It might also help you "cool off" until you're ready to talk respectfully with your mentor.
Reach out for help immediately.	There are certain situations when you should definitely talk with another adult, and not with your mentor. Be sure to ask a different person you trust for help in the following situations: → Your mentor tries to touch you in a way that makes you uncomfortable. → Your mentor is physically or emotionally abusive. → Your mentor talks to you in any way that makes you feel scared.

The whole point of mentoring is to form a relationship that makes you feel valuable, cared for, and safe. By working through conflicts with your mentor or with the help of other caring adults, you will have a stronger friendship that is more fun for both of you.

33

Saying Good-Bye to a Mentor

WAS IT SOMETHING I DID? NOW WHAT?

It is important to remember that every mentoring relationship ends at some point in time. In fact, your mentoring program may set up a limited amount of time for your mentoring relationship. Besides, it's normal for relationships to change over time.

Sometimes you grow away from people, and sometimes friends may talk less, but that doesn't mean the relationship was a failure. If your formal mentoring relationship is ending, you can try a few things to make the situation go as smoothly as possible.

IN GENERAL

➜ **Talk about it.** Even if the relationship is ending for positive reasons, one or both of you may still be feeling hurt or sad. Be thoughtful as you and your mentor share the feelings you are having.

➜ **If you want, invite your mentor to continue to be in your life.** You may not see each other as often, but offer to write letters, visit her, and invite her to participate in future milestones (a recital, game, graduation ceremony). Your mentor may be thrilled to be invited.

➜ **Talk about what you found most important and satisfying about your relationship** with your mentor, and encourage him to do the same.

➜ **Try not to completely cut yourself off from your mentor after the formal relationship ends.** Continue to let your mentor know how much she has meant to you through ongoing calls, letters, notes, e-mail messages, and visits when appropriate.

➜ **Let your mentor know how much he means to you.** Thank him for the opportunity to get to know him. Let him know how he has helped you change for the better.

IF YOU ARE THE ONE WHO NEEDS TO END THE RELATIONSHIP

➜ **Make sure you are certain that ending the formal mentoring relationship is the only option that will work.** Talk to your mentoring program staff about options to reduce the number of visits or other ways you can work in visits.

➜ **Be honest but careful.** You might be more comfortable talking about this issue with staff from the mentoring program there to help you. If your busy schedule is causing the need for change, don't leave your mentor thinking you don't have time for her. Instead, talk about the good things you like about your mentor, the changes she has made in your life, and the responsibilities that are taking your time (homework, school, other activities, time with friends and family).

IF YOUR MENTOR INITIATES THE ENDING OF THE RELATIONSHIP

➜ **Remember that sometimes it is healthy to outgrow a friendship and move forward.**

➜ **You may feel bad, but remember that this is not your fault.** Even if it hurts right now, you'll grow through this tough time.

➜ **Always remember that you are a worthwhile person** with gifts and strengths, and there will be other people in your life who will see these qualities, too.

Looking Back on Your Mentoring Experience

SO WHAT HAVE I GOTTEN OUT OF THIS RELATIONSHIP?

You've been through a lot with your mentor—the ups and downs, some fun activities, and maybe some tough discussions. As you look back at your time together or move toward a different kind of friend-ship, it is important for you to think about what you have gained from the mentoring experience.

Below are some questions to help you reflect on your mentoring experience. If you feel comfort-able doing so, discuss this handout and share your answers with your mentor.

Looking Back on My Mentoring Experience

What has having a mentor taught me about myself?	
What has having a mentor taught me about the world around me?	
Am I satisfied with the kind of mentee I have been?	
What three things am I proudest of?	

CONTINUES →

Am I sorry about anything in the relationship or how I handled it?	
When our relationship gets tough, what has kept me coming back to my mentor?	
What are my mentor's strengths?	
What has he or she taught me?	
What will I always remember about my relationship with my mentor?	
Looking back, was there anything that would have made this experience easier?	
Because of my mentoring experience, what will I do more, less, or differently in my life?	

MENTORS AND MENTEES TO USE TOGETHER

Your organization may already do substantial upfront work setting up mentor–mentee matches for a successful, thriving relationship. Effective recruitment, screening, matching, and training all go a long way in building a positive experience for mentees and mentors. One of the most challenging parts of your job may be helping matches build their relationship during their time together, when you may or may not be present to prompt them with ideas.

The following handouts will supply mentor–mentee matches with information, talking tips, and concrete activities for enriching their time together.

Whether they are working out schedules or struggling with stereotypes, matches will find that the Developmental Asset approach helps them face the challenges of mentoring as a team. As they work together toward common goals, they will develop a more productive and rewarding friendship.

You know the benefits of mentoring don't just come from the pairing of a mentee with a mentor. Rather, it's the quality of the relationship between the two that nurtures the positive development of mentees (and their mentors, too). Use these tools to help mentoring pairs achieve the meaningful results you know are possible.

35

Conversation Topics for Introducing Yourselves

Take turns asking each other to fill in the blanks after the items listed below.

BASIC STUFF ABOUT ME

My full name is . . .

_____

I was born in (country, city, state, province, or town) . . .

_____

My birthday is _____, and I am ____ years old.

I've lived in some of these places . . .

_____

One of my favorite things to do is . . .

_____

My least favorite thing to do is . . .

_____

When I was younger, I enjoyed . . .

_____

I spent a lot of time . . .

_____

When I was younger, the person I liked to be around was _____, because he or she . . .

_____

CONTINUES →

One adult who valued and accepted me was _____. Our relationship was . . .

_____

One of my best days was the day . . .

_____

One of my worst days was the day . . .

_____

School for me is/was . . .

_____

Some of the people I like to be around include . . .

_____

My favorite ice cream flavor(s) . . .

_____

Three more things I love to eat . . .

_____

Music I like to listen to . . .

_____

Names of the people who live with me . . .

_____

Sometimes I wish I could . . .

_____

Some things I like about where I live are . . .

_____

Some things I like about being the age I am are . . .

_____

This is how I'd describe my relationship with my parent(s) or guardian(s) . . .

_____

CONTINUES →

More than anything, I believe young people today need (list) . . .

_____

Parents and other adults need to try to understand that young people . . .

_____

When I think about my life today,

    I sometimes wonder if . . .

    _____

    I sometimes fear . . .

    _____

OUR NEW FRIENDSHIP

I'm interested in getting to know you because . . .

_____

I'm looking forward to . . .

_____

Some of the feelings or questions I have about my role in our friendship include . . .

_____

To make our times together fun and interesting for both of us, I'm willing to . . .

_____

When I look back on this experience a year from now, I hope I'll be able to say that I helped you to . . . (list)—and that you helped me to . . .

_____

_____

_____

36

Deeper Conversation Topics

Even if you two feel as if you have gotten to know each other pretty well, there is still plenty you can find out about each other by asking some deeper questions. Here are some ideas that will show you new sides of each other's personality and get you thinking about your own identity in the process.

Use scissors to cut out the topics listed below. Fold each slip of paper in half, and place all of them in a basket, a bowl, a jar, or a hat. Take turns choosing topics and answering questions for each other.

Tell me about your favorite teacher.	Talk about a time when you laughed so hard you thought you couldn't stop.	Name something you have always wished you could do. How could you make it happen?
Complete this sentence: One way I'd like to change the world is . . .	What is the biggest mistake you've made in your life? What did you learn from it?	What are three things about you that your friends would say make you a good friend to have?
If you could describe your ideal day, what would it be like?	How do you handle a situation when someone lies to you?	What is your biggest dream? What is the first step you can take toward achieving it?
What is a subject or topic that isn't taught in your school, but one you would really like to learn about?	What is one thing about your cultural heritage that you are really proud of?	What do you do when you disagree with rules you are supposed to follow?
When people first meet you, what do you think they see? What do you wish they would see in you?	If you could achieve only one great thing in your life, what would it be?	You fast-forward 50 years and discover a new holiday is named in your honor. What would people be celebrating about you?

37

Keeping Track of Our Scheduled Get-Togethers

Finding easy ways to schedule and keep track of your next visit can sometimes be tricky, especially if you both have busy schedules, or if either of you has unreliable access to a telephone in your home. Here are some tips for setting up reliable ways to schedule visits:

→ **Pick a regular day to meet.** Your mentoring program may have guidelines about when and where you meet. If your schedules allow for it, try selecting one day you will do something together each week. If you can also set the meetings at a predictable time, so much the better. (For example, you will pick up your mentee every Wednesday at 5:00 p.m.)

→ **Talk between visits.** Decide which of you will be in charge of calling the other person a few days before your next visit to check in about how things are going and remind each other of your next visit.

→ **Keep a calendar.** If there is a family calendar in the mentee's house, use it to write down your next visits. If there is not a family calendar in the house, mentors and mentees can look for a calendar that the parent(s) or caregiver(s) might like. Your mentoring program staff may even have calendars or supplies you can use to make a calendar together.

→ **Practice time management skills.** If you have day planners, pencil in your next few visits. Obviously, mentees need to check with their families to make sure the time will work. Make scheduling fun—draw pictures and use fun colors to "code" different kinds of activi-  ties. If one of you does not have much practice with maintaining a calendar or planner, work together to identify regular activities, family obligations, and other ways you occupy your time and plug those things into a day planner.

→ **Leave a note on the fridge.** Mentee, pick out a refrigerator magnet that you like. At the end of each visit, decide with your mentor and your family when the next visit will be. Write the date and time on a piece of paper, and put it on your home's refrigerator with the special magnet.

38

How Did Things Go Today?

Fill out this form after each of your visits. You can talk together about your reflections, or cut the page in half and fill out your sections separately. This process will help you think about what went well, what didn't, and how you can spend your time together in the future. If you like, you can save these pages and eventually bind them together into a book to enjoy as a reminder of your time together.

MENTOR'S REFLECTIONS

Date _____

Activities we did together

Things we talked about _____

Wishes or concerns that came up _____

The best thing that happened during our time together _____

What we'd like to do together in the future _____

MENTEE'S REFLECTIONS

Date _____

Activities we did together _____

Things we talked about _____

Wishes or concerns that came up _____

The best thing that happened during our time together _____

What we'd like to do together in the future _____

39

Identifying Common Interests

We can all find something we have in common with someone else, even someone who seems totally different from us. Maybe we both like chocolate chip cookie dough ice cream. Perhaps we both grew up in a single-parent family. However big or small our similarities, they are there—you just need to look for them.

Below are some ideas to help you find similarities.

Don't worry if you don't come up with much that overlaps at first. Eventually the two of you will have spent enough time together that you'll find more things you have in common, plus you'll have built some shared experiences you'll have in common as well. When you do find common interests, stop to chat more about why you like and dislike different things.

What Do We Have in Common?

	MENTOR'S ANSWERS	MENTEE'S ANSWERS
FAMILY		
Where I was born		
How many siblings I have		
Who raises/raised me		
Health concerns I have or have had		
Places I have lived		

CONTINUES →

	MENTOR'S ANSWERS	MENTEE'S ANSWERS
SCHOOL		
What kind of school I attend(ed)		
My favorite subjects		
My least favorite subjects		
Number of kids that are/were in my class		
Favorite teacher or adult at school		
INTERESTS		
Hobbies		
Places I like to go		
Places I've visited for vacation, work, family visits		

CONTINUES →

	MENTOR'S ANSWERS	MENTEE'S ANSWERS
Places I want to visit someday		
Games I like to play		
Things I'm good at doing		
Things I want to get better at doing		
Favorite animals		
Favorite types of music		
Favorite types of books		
Favorite movies or television shows		
Favorite foods		
Least favorite foods		

CONTINUES →

	MENTOR'S ANSWERS	MENTEE'S ANSWERS
VALUES		
I believe strongly in . . .		
I want to change the world so that . . .		
I think money can be good because . . .		
I think money can be bad because . . .		
FUTURE		
What kind of career do I want someday?		
What kind of family do I hope to have?		
What do I want people to say about me at my 100th birthday party?		

40

Reflecting on the Asset Categories

Developmental Assets describe the positive qualities, experiences, and opportunities young people need to grow up to be caring, healthy adults. These assets fall into the eight categories listed below. To get a better understanding of each other, use these questions to talk together about how each of you experiences these assets in your life.

SUPPORT

- Where or to whom do you turn for advice? Are there people who come to you for advice?

- Do the important people in your life encourage you, help you, pay attention to you, and comfort you or defend you when you need it? Do you do these things for other people?

- Do you have enough relationships with people who really listen to you? Who are those people?

EMPOWERMENT

- Where do you turn for help when you don't feel safe? Who protects you? Who looks to you for protection?

- Do people trust you to be reliable and dependable? In what ways are you a leader? In what ways are you a follower or a supporter? What kinds of decisions can you make alone?

- Who are your role models? Are you a good role model for your friends and for people younger than you?

BOUNDARIES AND EXPECTATIONS

- Why can't everyone just do what they want to do? Why are there rules and limits?

- Are the adults around you good role models? In what ways?

- Do others expect a lot from you? Do they ever expect too much from you? Do you expect a lot from yourself?

CONSTRUCTIVE USE OF TIME

- Do you like to be with large groups of people? Or do you prefer spending time alone or with just one or two people? How does that affect the kinds of activities you enjoy?

- Are there any places near your home where you could go to join in with others who are doing interesting things? How can you find out more about these places and activities?

- Have you ever dreamed of being a musician, an artist, an athlete, a scientist, a writer, or an actor? How could you start making those dreams come true?

CONTINUES →

COMMITMENT TO LEARNING

- Do you believe you can learn anything if you set your mind to it? What kinds of things are easy for you to learn? What kinds of things are harder?

- Do you do well at school and/or at your job? Do you *want* to do well at school and/or your job?

- What kinds of things are you good at? Athletics? Dance? Organizing? Playing music? Making jokes? Building a great vocabulary? Doing math? Memorizing facts? Fixing cars? Working on computers? Baking fancy desserts?

POSITIVE VALUES

- Whom do you care about? Who cares about you?

- What do you believe in? What do you think life is all about? What is the best way to live? How do you know you're a good person?

- Do you take responsibility for your actions, or do you blame others? How often do you say, "It's not my fault"? Do you take responsibility for your choices? For your opinions?

SOCIAL COMPETENCIES

- How many friends do you have who are of the same race or background as you? How many friends do you have who are of a different race or background than you? How about friends of a different gender or a different religion?

- Do people have to agree with you to be your friends? How do you stay friends with people when you have disagreements or differences of opinion?

- Do you try to imagine how other people feel when you're deciding on actions to take? Do you talk to them and listen to them so that you understand each other? How can you learn more about being a good friend?

POSITIVE IDENTITY

- How do you know your life has a purpose? Do you get to choose the purpose, or is the purpose something you're supposed to discover? Does everyone have the same purpose? Are some purposes good and some not so good?

- If you close your eyes, can you imagine your future? What will your family be like? Where will you live? What kinds of work will you do? Who will be your closest friends?

- Can you control everything that happens to you? Can you control anything that happens to you? Who else has control over parts of your life? Do you feel as if they are teaching you and helping you, or are they stopping you from making your own decisions?

41

Bridging Generational Differences

Whether there is a five-year age difference between mentor and mentee or a 50-year age difference, there is a chance that one or both of you is feeling a little uncomfortable with the fact that you are in different stages of your lives. Some of this could be because of the myths or stereotypes you may have heard about adults and young people through the media and from other people you know. A stereotype is an idea you believe about a whole group of people without thinking about them as individuals. Have you ever heard these things?

ADULTS ARE . . .

- strict,

- forgetful of what it's like to be young, or

- disrespectful of young people's ideas and abilities.

YOUNG PEOPLE ARE . . .

- lazy,

- irresponsible, or

- self-centered.

Instead of falling back on these stereotypes, try not to jump to conclusions about an individual. When you are getting to know each other, listen for what the other person does, knows, believes, and has the possibility to become. Below is a list of conversation starters that can help you get to know each other, to better understand each other's experience as young people, and to "bust" some of the myths we have about each other's generations.

FAMILY

- What were/are some of the ground rules your family had/has?

- What kind of traditions did/does your family honor?

- How old were you before you were allowed to . . .

    . . . stay over at a friend's house?

    . . . watch a scary movie?

    . . . get your ears pierced?

    . . . go to a dance at school?

    . . . go on a date?

    . . . drive?

SCHOOL

- What was/is the dress code at your school?

- What major world events happened while you were in school? How did your teachers help students talk about them?

- What kinds of traditions did/does your school have?

- What sports did/do you play?

- What other activities did/do you do?

- What classes did/do you take? How were/are they meant to prepare you for a career path?

CONTINUES →

TECHNOLOGY

- In what format did/do you listen to music as a young person (e.g. vinyl records, 8-tracks, cassettes, CDs)?

- Did you/do you have computers to work on at school? What were/are they like?

- How did/do you communicate with friends and relatives (e.g. writing letters, talking on phones with cords, sending e-mail, and instant messaging)?

- What was/is the television you had growing up like (e.g. remote controls, number of channels)?

ENTERTAINMENT

- What kind of music did/do you and your friends listen to? Why did/do you like it?

- How did/does your family feel about the music you like?

- What television shows did/do you watch?

- Which celebrities were/are popular with you and your friends?

- What concerts have you attended?

- What were/are your favorite movies as a teen?

- How much did/does it cost to go to a movie theater? What was/is the theater like?

FASHION

- What were/are some of the important fashion trends you've experienced as a teen?

- How did/do people style their hair?

- What were/are you not allowed to wear by your family and/or school?

LOCAL, NATIONAL, AND WORLD EVENTS

- What was/is going on in the world that really made/makes you think about life and your role in it?

- What events happened/happen in your neighborhood or community that made/make you think about life and your role in it?

JOBS

- What was your first job? How much did/do you make an hour?

- What's the weirdest job you've ever had?

42

Avoiding Stereotypes

Getting to know and like people requires you to see them for who they really are. This seems obvious and straightforward, but it is easy to get caught up in what people have, where they're from, what they look like, or how old they are and to assume things about them based on very little information, rather than actually finding out what they are like, what they enjoy doing, and what their hopes and dreams for the future look like.

It is very possible that the two of you live in different parts of town (or in different cities altogether), grew up in different kinds of families, or have different cultural or ethnic backgrounds. That doesn't mean you can't find common ground and even enjoy each other's company.

The Peace Corps Web site (www.peacecorps. gov) offers advice to teachers and students on how to avoid stereotyping others. These tips also work well for mentors and mentees.

❶ Think about or share opposite examples when someone makes a sweeping generalization.

Instead of saying: My mentor can't be cool because she drives a minivan.

You can say: My mentor may drive a minivan, but she listens to great music on the radio.

❷ Give specific rather than general information about people.

Example: My mentee loves to read and does well in school. In his spare time, he likes playing basketball and hanging out with friends. Our favorite place to eat together is at the local Chinese restaurant.

❸ Point out the good or positive things about others.

Example: My mentee always finds the time to finish her homework after helping care for her brothers and sisters.

❹ Share cultural information.

Example: My mentor fasts during Ramadan. He showed me the Islamic calendar and explained why Ramadan happens at a different time each year.

❺ Actively question (even just to yourself) the reliability of the source of information.

Example: I wonder if John really knows what people who live in a rural area are like. He was only there a few times. Maybe he or someone he knows just had a bad experience.

❻ If you disagree, do so politely.

Example: Really, I just don't agree with you that girls don't do as well as boys in math. That hasn't been true in our class.

❼ Point out that what may be true for some is not necessarily true for all.

Example: I know some people in my mentee's neighborhood are not employed. However, most of his neighbors are looking for jobs or already hold down two or more jobs to make ends meet.

❽ Wait before making a judgment.

Think to yourself: That girl seems really stuck-up to me, but I'd better wait to form an opinion about her. Maybe she just doesn't speak English very well. Or maybe she's shy.

43

Exploring Our Differences and Similarities

Use two copies of this handout to talk about the stereotypes people might have about each of you and to talk about the individual strengths you have apart from the stereotypes. Fill it out or think about your answers by yourself, then talk with each other about your responses.

Characteristics	The Group My Mentor/ Mentee Fits	Stereotypes about People in This Group	What My Mentor/Mentee Is Really Like	What I Have in Common with My Mentor/Mentee
Age (teenager, young adult, middle aged, elder)				
Gender				
Neighborhood				
Race/ethnicity				
Family structure				

44

Free and Low-Cost Activity Ideas

Looking for new things to do that don't cost a lot of money? There are plenty of options for you—inside or outside, around home or out and about, physically active or relaxing—take your pick! Below are just a few ideas for things you can do together that don't necessarily require spending a lot of money.

General Activities We'd Like to Try

Mentor Mentee

- ☐ ☐ Cooking
- ☐ ☐ Having lunch together
- ☐ ☐ Going bargain shopping
- ☐ ☐ Playing board games
- ☐ ☐ Playing video games
- ☐ ☐ Playing card games
- ☐ ☐ Spending time on a farm
- ☐ ☐ Making crafts or art
- ☐ ☐ Attending a family gathering
- ☐ ☐ Going to a book signing or author reading
- ☐ ☐ Working on cars or bikes
- ☐ ☐ Scrapbooking
- ☐ ☐ Talking on the phone
- ☐ ☐ Taking care of pets
- ☐ ☐ Eating ice cream
- ☐ ☐ Learning photography
- ☐ ☐ Doing simple building projects
- ☐ ☐ Learning how to knit or quilt
- ☐ ☐ Visiting each other's faith community
- ☐ ☐ Figuring out how to program a VCR, fix a computer, or some other appliance
- ☐ ☐ Volunteering together for a local cause
- ☐ ☐ Making stationery together, then sending each other notes on it over the course of the next year

Academic, Career, and Life Skills–Focused Activities We'd Like to Try

Mentor Mentee

- ☐ ☐ Doing homework
- ☐ ☐ Reading
- ☐ ☐ Working on a résumé
- ☐ ☐ Talking about career interests
- ☐ ☐ Talking about education possibilities, beyond high school
- ☐ ☐ Visiting a local technical school, community college, or university
- ☐ ☐ Working on college applications
- ☐ ☐ Working on financial aid applications
- ☐ ☐ Practicing job interview skills
- ☐ ☐ Learning to balance a checkbook
- ☐ ☐ Going to a library
- ☐ ☐ Investigating the pros and cons of credit cards
- ☐ ☐ Taking a community education class together
- ☐ ☐ Looking for jobs or internships
- ☐ ☐ Touring the mentor's workplace
- ☐ ☐ Talking about balancing work and life
- ☐ ☐ Talking about living within one's means

CONTINUES →

Sports and Physical Activities We'd Like to Try

Mentor Mentee

- ☐ ☐ Swimming
- ☐ ☐ Bike riding
- ☐ ☐ Rollerblading
- ☐ ☐ Bowling
- ☐ ☐ Canoeing or boating
- ☐ ☐ Sledding
- ☐ ☐ Going to a park
- ☐ ☐ Fishing
- ☐ ☐ Playing catch
- ☐ ☐ Horseback riding
- ☐ ☐ Hunting
- ☐ ☐ Learning karate
- ☐ ☐ Snowboarding or skiing

Events and Activities That May Cost More Money That We'd Like to Try

Mentor Mentee

- ☐ ☐ Going to a play
- ☐ ☐ Going to a museum
- ☐ ☐ Attending a poetry slam
- ☐ ☐ Going to an amusement park
- ☐ ☐ Going to a county or state fair
- ☐ ☐ Attending a community or neighborhood parade or festival
- ☐ ☐ Attending a fund-raiser for a school, congregation, or other cause
- ☐ ☐ Attending a sporting event together
- ☐ ☐ Going to a concert together
- ☐ ☐ Visiting the zoo
- ☐ ☐ Going to a movie
- ☐ ☐ Going to a show together (like a flower show or an auto show)

A Year's Worth of Mentoring Activities

Polly Roach of the Mentoring Partnership of Minnesota shares 52 weeks' worth of mentoring activities, one for each week of the year. Use the blank spaces to plan your own ideas.

JANUARY

Here are a few ideas:

- Celebrate National Mentoring Month.
- Make your New Year's resolutions and set your mentoring goals.
- Develop a Web site.
- Attend a hockey game or figure skating show.
- Write thank-you notes for holiday presents.

Your ideas:

-
-

FEBRUARY

Here are a few ideas:

- Rent each other's favorite movies.
- Read the same book and discuss it.
- Go sledding.
- Talk about your first job.

Your ideas:

-
-

MARCH

Here are a few ideas:

- Go to a high school basketball game.
- Make plans for spring break.

- Talk about planning a career.
- Set goals for physical fitness an d work out together.

Your ideas:

-
-

APRIL

Here are a few ideas:

- Go to a baseball game.
- Plant seeds for a garden.
- Talk about taxes.
- Tour a college campus and learn about how to prepare for enrollment.

Your ideas:

-
-

MAY

Here are a few ideas:

- Go to a high school play.
- Work on a résumé.
- Plant a tree.
- Go fishing.

Your ideas:

-
-

CONTINUES →

JUNE

Here are a few ideas:

- Look for a summer job or internship.
- Go to a free outdoor concert.
- Develop a portfolio to showcase skills.
- Shoot some hoops.
- Go outside and take pictures together.
- Build a birdhouse or craft project.

Your ideas:

-
-

JULY

Here are a few ideas:

- Talk about news and current events.
- Go to a parade.
- Search for great fireworks displays.
- Watch a movie with a mentoring theme and discuss it.
- Talk about how to look for a job.

Your ideas:

-
-

AUGUST

Here are a few ideas:

- Go to the beach.
- Make dinner together.
- Share a talent or teach a skill.
- Talk about planning a budget.

Your ideas:

-
-

SEPTEMBER

Here are a few ideas:

- Prepare for the school year.

- Tour your city/town.
- Visit an orchard.
- Volunteer for a fund-raiser or service project together.

Your ideas:

-
-

OCTOBER

Here are a few ideas:

- Go to a football game.
- Tackle some homework.
- Talk about what it takes to succeed.
- Go on a haunted hayride.

Your ideas:

-
-

NOVEMBER

Here are a few ideas:

- Take a walk together.
- Talk about elections and politics.
- Volunteer at a food shelf or shelter.
- Write a story or poem together.

Your ideas:

-
-

DECEMBER

Here are a few ideas:

- Help make creative presents for each other's families.
- Bake cookies together.
- Make a scrapbook of all the different things you have done.
- Talk about the future.

Your ideas:

-

46

Setting and Reaching Goals

Here is a worksheet to help both of you find ways to set goals and identify steps toward reaching those goals. Use the blank spaces to help each other brainstorm ways to achieve your individual goals.

Experiences I Might Want in My Life	What I Might Need to Know About	Ways I Could Find Out about These Things	What Else I Might Need to Make It Happen
To go to trade school, college, or university	■ What I like to do ■ What I'm good at ■ What kinds of schools are available and their cost ■ How to complete admission and loan applications	■ Ask people with interesting jobs to let me "shadow" them for a day ■ Join clubs to find out what interests me ■ Get help from a librarian or career counselor to find out about schools	■ A quiet place to study ■ Someone to take me on a college tour
To be a professional athlete	■ What skills I need to play a particular sport ■ What the sport's rules are ■ How to stay motivated ■ How to manage the money I make ■ How the muscles of my body work	■ Take physical education classes and join sports teams ■ Talk with coaches ■ Read autobiographies of great sports figures ■ Study math and accounting to learn about money management	■ Someone with a driver's license to give me rides to and from practice

CONTINUES →

Experiences I Might Want in My Life	What I Might Need to Know About	Ways I Could Find Out about These Things	What Else I Might Need to Make It Happen

FAMILIES OF MENTEES

R esearch shows that the presence of a supportive family in a mentee's life can significantly enhance the effectiveness of the mentoring relationship. However, parents and guardians may not fully grasp just how much their encouragement (or lack of it) can influence the relationship's success. Preparing families to contribute positively to the mentoring experience is another important challenge you face as a program provider.

The following set of handouts will help families see how valuable their contributions are. As parents or caregivers learn more about the role of a mentor and this opportunity to help their child grow, they may learn to welcome, celebrate, and thank the new friend in their child's life. Even if your program serves a population with limited family involvement, the Developmental Assets are useful in helping parents or caregivers recognize that mentoring can be a powerful strategy for enhancing their child's positive development.

Because you probably have less contact with them, the families of mentees may be one of your toughest audiences to reach. The tools offered here will open the door to their supportive involvement. When families identify themselves as an important part of a child's mentoring team, the experience becomes more rewarding and meaningful for everyone involved.

47

The Mentor's Role in Your Child's Life

So What's a Mentor Really Supposed to Do?

Finding a mentor for your child is a fantastic way to be a good caregiver. Mentors can provide positive attention to young people, expose them to new experiences, and model healthy behaviors. You have the wisdom to know that your child needs as many caring adults in her or his life as possible. All kids need that kind of support, and your child is lucky to have a family who understands that and has made it happen.

But you might be wondering what exactly this new person in your child's life is supposed to do. Where are the lines between a mentor's responsibility and what you as a parent or caregiver should be doing? Below are some general guidelines.

A MENTOR IS . . .

. . . a friend. Like peer friendships, mentors and mentees do things together that are fun and engaging. They teach each other. They help each other. They're honest with each other. And sometimes they need to have hard conversations about concerns they may have.

. . . a role model. A mentor should try to set a good example for how your child can live his life. This is not the same as being perfect. Rather, mentors should admit their imperfections and share their strengths.

. . . someone your child can talk to. Your child may tell her mentor things she does not feel comfortable telling you or anyone else. Sometimes she may tell the mentor about hopes, dreams, or fears. Other times she may reveal mistakes she has made. The mentor's role is to be supportive of your child as a person with many life possibilities, regardless of the kinds of actions or attitudes she confides.

. . . another person who is proud of your child. Your child's mentor should be able to see all the gifts he has and help him learn and grow. The mentor can help him channel his gifts toward actions that make a positive difference to others in your family, neighborhood, school, or community.

CONTINUES →

A MENTOR IS NOT . . .

. . . a mentor to the family. The mentor's role is to provide special attention to one child, your child. While getting acquainted with you and your child's siblings can help the mentor better understand your child, his energy and attention should only be focused on your child.

. . . a social worker or doctor. If your child tells the mentor about experiences or health conditions that concern her, the mentor may turn to professionals for help. It is not a mentor's responsibility to try to address conditions or situations that require professional help.

. . . a savior. Certainly the mentor's support can help your child overcome hurdles. But mentors should know that all young people—regardless of their circumstances—have gifts and talents that make them more than just "receivers" of services. The mentor should treat your child as though he has much to offer to the world, because he does.

Your role in your child's mentoring relationship is also important. The more supportive you are, the more likely their relationship will be a healthy and successful one.

YOU CAN BE . . .

. . . a good listener. Share in your child's excitement and concerns about her mentor.

. . . a schedule keeper. Help your child plan time with his mentor, and find ways to remind him about upcoming meetings.

. . . a voice of gratitude. Help your child show her appreciation to her mentor. Find ways to show your appreciation.

48

Supporting Your Child's Relationship with a Mentor

What Can I Do to Help Make This Work?

By involving your son or daughter in a mentoring relationship, you have taken a very important step to making sure your child gets what he or she needs in life. Every young person benefits from having another caring adult in his life—someone who supports your child, believes in him, and can be another person your child turns to when he's having a tough time—so kudos to you for welcoming a mentor into your child's life!

A good mentor–mentee relationship takes time to develop. Just like the start of any friendship, the mentor and your child will need to spend some time getting to know each other. They may encounter difficulties or misunderstandings along the way. There will be ups and downs.

You as a parent or caregiver can play a very important role in helping their friendship grow and develop, regardless of whether or not you have much direct contact with the mentor.

Here are some tips to help you support your child's new mentoring relationship:

- **Be positive.** Let your child see that you are happy she has a mentor in her life. When your child tells you about her visit with her mentor, listen for the positive experiences, even if your child doesn't seem very excited about the visit. (For example, you might point out, "Well, it sounds as if you two have some things in common. Getting to know someone isn't always easy, but give it time.")

- **Tell your child the positive skills and behaviors you see her developing as a result of having a mentor,** and let him know that you are pleased with those changes. ("I've noticed that since you started hanging out with Joe, you've gotten your homework done on time more often. I'm proud of you!")

- **Let the mentor know how much you appreciate that she is a part of your child's life.** An occasional card or just telling her "thank you" can do much to make the mentor feel she matters.

- Encourage your child to **show his mentor that he appreciates him.**

- If you are present when your child and mentor get together (for example, during pickup and drop-off), **be available but not overbearing.** Show your interest by asking some questions, but try not to make demands.

- **Share feedback from your child with the mentoring program's staff.** If you are allowed to talk with the mentor privately, check in occasionally and see how the relationship is going.

- **Help your child remember when her next visit with her mentor is scheduled.** Help her use a calendar or day planner to keep track of visits with her mentor, as well as other activities going on in her life. Try to be as flexible as possible with the scheduling of activities.

CONTINUES →

- **Give your child's mentor copies of school calendars** so that he knows about time off for holidays, opening and closing days of the school year, special events, and other considerations.

- The program may take care of this, but it's always a good idea to **provide your child's mentor with emergency contact information** for someone with a phone, just in case something happens and the mentor cannot reach you.

- **Let the mentoring program's staff or your child's mentor know if there has been a change or incident in your child's home life that the mentor should know about.** Did you two have a particularly bad fight recently? Has there been a death in the family? Are there financial stresses in the household right now? Is one of her siblings in need of extra attention right now? This kind of information will help the program and the mentor to more effectively support your child. You may also want to make some suggestions about how the mentor can be supportive in these situations.

- **Be prepared in the back of your mind for the inevitable end to the mentoring relationship.** Every mentoring relationship ends at some point. Some mentoring programs are designed so that the mentor and mentee are together for a limited time. If the relationship is strong and life remains relatively stable for the mentor and your child, it may not end until your child graduates from high school. The fact that your child's mentor has gone through a recruitment, training, and screening process is a good sign that she is committed to staying involved with your child over a significant period of time. Unfortunately, sometimes things change in either the mentor's or your child's life that are out of either one's control, and a relationship may need to end prematurely. Remember that sometimes a mentoring relationship ends in a healthy way for good reasons. For example, your child may get swamped with school activities like band and sports, or the mentor may be busy with a new baby. No matter what the reason, you can be ready to listen and provide extra support when the relationship ends.

- **Remember that the mentor is not going to replace you.** You are still your child's parent, and nothing will ever change that. The mentor can complement and reinforce what you are doing as a parent, helping you be even more effective.

49

Mixed Feelings

What If My Child Seems to Like the Mentor Better Than Me?

Sure, you're already convinced that having a mentor will be a wonderful experience for your child; however, you may also feel a little worried that the mentor has it easier than you, the parent or caregiver. The mentor's main role is to be your child's friend, someone who gets to swoop in for a few hours a week to have fun with your child. You are still left with the day-to-day necessities of being your child's parent, like making sure he does his homework, stays healthy, is well behaved, and completes household chores. Even when you know how important your role is, it can be difficult to feel like "the bad guy" who enforces all of the rules and doesn't get to have fun.

It's very natural that a parent or caregiver of a child who is involved with a mentor may feel a little jealous or worry about losing some of the child's affection to this new person in her life. Share your feelings with the staff at the mentoring program, and ask if they have any advice for you. If you start to worry that your child will like her mentor better than she does you, remind yourself of these things:

- **Young people who have more caring adults in their life do better in school, get involved in fewer risky behaviors, and are more likely to become caring, healthy, and responsible adults.** Research shows that your child's successful involvement with a mentor can boost her or his odds of becoming an adult who has numerous options in life, rather than one who has engaged in negative behaviors that close doors to future opportunities.

- **The mentor can never replace you.** You are still your child's primary caregiver, and nothing will ever change that. When your child feels affection toward another person, that doesn't mean his love for you is lessened. You and your child have a history together that cannot be replaced by someone, however caring, who spends a few hours a week with your child.

- **The mentor can actually strengthen what you are doing** as a family by reinforcing your rules, helping you be even more effective. If you don't communicate with the mentor directly, ask program staff to pass along your family's rules about curfews, eating sweets, watching movies, or other issues that concern you.

- **The mentor may improve the relationship between you and your child.** As your child talks things over with another adult, she may learn new communication skills. A caring mentor may also be able to help her recognize positive things about her family.

- **You can set aside your own special time together.** When you and your child find time to have fun with each other, you may feel better about the time he spends with his mentor. Even if you simply make dinner together, you can spend the time telling jokes and having meaningful conversations.

50

What Are Developmental Assets?

What Does My Child Need to Succeed?

People become parents or family caregivers in so many different ways: by chance or choice, by accident or against all odds, when very young or "well seasoned." Regardless of your story, you have an opportunity to be a true hero—to have a positive influence that will last throughout your child's lifetime. Welcoming a mentor into your child's life is just one way in which you can make a difference.

Many of the small and big things you do for your child are included in a list researchers have defined called the Developmental Assets framework. The framework consists of 40 commonsense, positive experiences and qualities youth need to be successful. (If you haven't received a copy of the complete list and would like to learn more, you can visit www.search-institute.org/assets/assetlists.) Parents and mentors can be important partners in building assets with and for young people.

The Developmental Assets are divided into eight categories. Strong evidence shows that by focusing on these eight specific areas of development, you can help guide your kids on productive paths through life. As you read through the categories below, remember that, while you are critical to building these good things with your children, you do not have to do this all alone. Think of ways in which other adults, including your child's mentor, can play a role in building these positive aspects of life with and for your child.

CONTINUES →

EXTERNAL ASSETS

SUPPORT—Kids need families who show that they love their children and will stand by them, no matter what. Children need to know that your love for them has no limits, that it is unconditional. Such love does not mean saying yes to whatever your kids want—you can still show your love by saying no. Instead, it means never withholding your love for them. Giving your children unconditional love shows them that they belong and are important.

EMPOWERMENT—Children need parents or caregivers who make it clear that children, especially their own, are valued and valuable just as they are. Make your home a safe place, and remind your children that they have something meaningful to contribute to the larger community as well as to the family.

BOUNDARIES AND EXPECTATIONS— Children need families who have high yet realistic expectations for their children, and who set and uphold clear limits about what is acceptable and unacceptable behavior. Kids do better in life when rules are clear, consistent, and fair. Setting limits is often hard; what parent doesn't dread being the target of a child's anger? But saying no at times can be an important way to help your kids learn how to succeed in the world. Similarly, you can more readily help children be the best they can be when your expectations for them are both high and reasonable.

CONSTRUCTIVE USE OF TIME—Children need families who help them balance school, activities, time with friends, and time at home. Constructive use of time means interacting with other supportive and caring people, including time at home just being with family. Constructive use of time is also about having chances to explore and express creativity, to learn and develop new skills, and to have fun with good friends.

INTERNAL ASSETS

COMMITMENT TO LEARNING—Young people need families who encourage and model a love of learning. A love for learning means the desire to succeed in school (and not just for good grades); it also means your children believe in their own abilities and want to do well.

POSITIVE VALUES—Kids need families who talk about and model basic values such as honesty, trust, and responsibility. It's part of a parent or caregiver's job to teach children how to treat other people. You can do this by letting your kids know what's important to you, what you value. The way your children think is also influenced by the actions of people they admire; in fact, they may be more influenced by the good things you *do* than by the good words you *say*.

SOCIAL COMPETENCIES—Young people need families who instill in their children an interest in and comfort with many kinds of people, and who help them develop strong skills to relate respectfully to everyone and show consideration for the rights of others. To help children learn how to enjoy and appreciate others day to day, whatever the circumstances, parents are wise to teach and model that *all* people matter. Children learn to care for others by learning what it means to care for themselves.

POSITIVE IDENTITY—Children need parents and caregivers who nurture their self-esteem, feeling of control over their own lives, and sense of hope. A young child's sense of happiness flourishes in large part from seeing herself or himself as a reflection of the adults in the family. What are your children seeing when they look at you? If your children see you as a parent who lives each day full of hope, striving to be your best, they will begin to develop their own sense of personal power and happiness.

51

Staying in the Loop with Your Child's Mentoring Experience

How Can I Stay "In the Know" with My Child and Her or His Mentor?

Hopefully you and your child communicate well, but sometimes you may find that it is not always easy to get information out of a young person. Have you ever had this conversation with your child?

"How was school?"

"Fine."

"What did you do?"

"Nothing."

"Did you learn anything new?"

"No."

"What are your friends up to these days?"

"Nothing."

Even if your child is willing to communicate, there are things you can do to make your conversations more effective. Here are a few ideas for finding out more about your child's relationship with her or his mentor.

- **Ask your child questions.** Whether or not your child acts as if she wants to talk to you, asking her about what is going on in her life shows her you care.

- **Keep asking.** If you ask after every visit your child has with his mentor, regardless of the reaction you get, your child will at least know you care about what is happening in the relationship.

- **Talk about safety.** Check to be sure that your child's mentoring program conducts background checks on volunteers. Once your child has been matched with a mentor, ask the program staff to share information about seat belt use during car trips, alcohol consumption in front of your child, or any other specific issues that concern you.

- **Use open-ended questions or statements** when talking with your child about what's going on with her mentor. These are questions or statements that can't be answered with just a yes or a no. Use statements like these in your conversation:

  – What did you do with your mentor tonight?

  – What was the best part of your visit with him or her?

  – What kind of person is your mentor?

  – What are you planning to do the next time you get together?

  – That sounds interesting. Tell me more about . . .

- If you see the mentor, **ask for her or his perspective on what the pair has been up to.** You might learn different details your child didn't think to share.

52

Supporting Your Child through the Phases of a Mentoring Relationship

WHAT CAN I DO TO HELP?

Every relationship—friendships, parent–child, siblings, marriage—goes through different stages or cycles. The same holds true for the friendship between a mentor and your child. At each stage, mentors and mentees may be experiencing some common anxieties and behaviors that reflect what is happening in their relationship at that stage. By understanding what children might be going through at each stage, you can help them experience fewer bumps in the road.

The Big Brothers Big Sisters program of the Greater Twin Cities in Minneapolis, Minnesota, outlines four stages in the growth cycle of a mentoring match, as well as some helpful strategies for successfully navigating each stage.

❶ Beginning the relationship—In this stage the mentor and your child are testing the waters with each other. Your child may feel nervous or wary, and she may be on her best behavior for her mentor. She may also get frustrated if things don't go as expected. Your child's mentor may want to "fix" everything. The mentor may also be finding himself adjusting his initial expectations about being a mentor, once he's experienced it for real. Both of them may be trying to bridge age, cultural, and lifestyle differences in each other.

Strategies for this stage:

- Show you are willing to listen to your child about what's happening in the mentoring relationship.

- Be aware of your own feelings about age, cultural, and lifestyle differences. Try to avoid stereotyping people or making assumptions about what they must think of you.

- Try to be nonjudgmental.

- Reach out, be available.

❷ Building trust—Now that the two of them know each other better and have some shared experiences under their belts, the mentor and your child will feel greater trust. Your child may be coming out of his shell, feeling better about himself, or simply more confident because the mentor has demonstrated that he cares. As a result, your child may share more information with his mentor. He may start to rely on his mentor more for support and validation in this stage, possibly to the point of becoming overdependent. At this stage, the mentor may be experiencing more satisfaction with the mentoring relationship. However, he also may be feeling overwhelmed by the extent of the issues faced by your child.

Strategies for this stage:

- Be patient, and encourage your child to be patient as well.

- Expect some setbacks.

- Set limits.

- Continue to be consistent and reliable.

CONTINUES →

❸ Testing the relationship—Now that rapport and trust are built, it is typical for your child to start testing boundaries in the relationship. Deep down, she may still want to see just how much staying power this relationship really has. Your child may make inappropriate requests of her mentor. She may even show resentment or hostility toward her. The mentor may start resenting what seems like negative behavior, and she might also feel caught in the middle between your child, your family, or other service providers.

Strategies for this stage:

- Remind your child about appropriate behaviors and limits when he is with his mentor.

- Continue to treat your child as capable.

- Let your child's mentor know how much you appreciate all she does for your child. A call or card may be just what she needs to help her through what might be a more difficult time in the mentoring relationship.

❷ Increasing independence—Having come through the trust-building and the relationship-testing stages, you may find your child becoming less dependent on his mentor and finding other sources of support. On the upside, you might also see increased feelings of self-worth in your child by now. However, setbacks are still possible during this stage as your child may take bigger risks in his life and in his relationship with his mentor. As a result of all of this, your child's mentor may feel discouraged or less needed during this stage.

Strategies for this stage:

- Point out the shifts in behavior you are observing and reinforce your child's efforts to seek support from others.

- Continue to support your child while encouraging independence.

- Expect some setbacks as a natural part of this stage.

- Continue to let your child's mentor know how much you appreciate all she does for your child. Assure her that she is making a positive difference in your child's life.

53

Helping Your Child Say Good-Bye to a Mentor

HOW SHOULD I HANDLE THIS SITUATION?

It is important to remember that every mentoring relationship will end at some point in time. In fact, the mentoring program may set a limited amount of time for your child's mentoring relationship. Although you may not be able to make this transition completely easy or painless for your child, below are a few things you can try to make the situation as smooth as possible.

In General

- **Avoid the blame game.** Remember that most relationships change over time, and that sometimes it is healthy to end a relationship and move forward. Acknowledge that this may be hard and sad for your child, but remember to focus on the positive things that have come out of the relationship. Modeling this positive focus will help your child do the same.

- **If appropriate, encourage your child to invite her mentor to continue to be in her life.** Encourage her to write letters, visit, and invite the mentor to participate in future milestones (a recital, game, graduation ceremony). Try to encourage your child not to cut ties with her mentor completely after the formal relationship ends. Encourage your child to send letters and e-mails, and to make calls to stay in touch with her mentor and remind her how important she still is to your child.

- **Encourage your child to talk** about what he found most important and satisfying about his relationship with his mentor.

- **Let your child's mentor know how much you appreciate what she has done for your child.** Do this even if the mentor is the one initiating the end of the formal mentoring relationship.

- **Encourage your child to let his mentor know how much he means to him.** Have your child thank his mentor for the opportunity to get to know him, and let him know how he has helped your child change for the better.

If Your Child Is the One Who Needs to End the Relationship

- **Make sure you and your child are certain that ending the formal mentoring relationship is the only workable option.** Talk to your mentoring program staff about options to reduce the number of visitations or other ways you can work in visits.

- **Coach him to be honest but careful.** For example, if lack of time is the issue causing the need for change, you don't want to leave the mentor thinking your child doesn't have time for him. Rather, help your child talk with his mentor about the good things he has liked about him, the positive changes he has made in your child's life, and the other responsibilities your child is facing (homework, school, other activities, time with friends and family).

CONTINUES →

If the Mentor Initiates the End of the Relationship

- If your child is feeling badly, remind your child that **this outcome is not her fault.**

- Remind your child that **he is a worthwhile person with gifts and strengths.**

- Explain that **sometimes the ending of a relationship can be a healthy thing in the long run.** It may hurt to end the mentoring relationship right now, but he will get through this in time. Learning to handle these situations positively is a valuable part of growing up.

resources from search institute

Below is a summary of Search Institute's resources that can help you enhance your mentoring program, as well as support materials you can provide to mentors, mentees, and families of mentees. At the time of first publication of *Mentoring for Meaningful Results,* these resources were all available. Please check the online catalog (www.search-institute.org/catalog) or contact client services staff at 1-877-240-7250 to obtain further information.

RESOURCES FOR MENTORING PROGRAMS

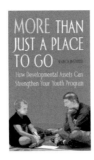

More Than Just a Place to Go: How Developmental Assets Can Strengthen Your Youth Program (video)

Based on three different out-of-school programs in three different states and settings, this video shows how to create and foster an asset-based environment, staff, and program for young people. Inspirational and informative, this video offers firsthand accounts from program administrators, staff, volunteers, parents, community leaders, and youth participants as well. The video highlights specific asset-building programs, practices, and strategies that can be used to help motivate and strengthen any out-of-school program. A great tool for in-service and new staff training.

More Than Just a Place to Go: How Developmental Assets Can Strengthen Your Youth Program (book)

The companion to the inspirational and informative *More Than Just a Place to Go* video, this book encourages youth programs to integrate assets into their current programs. This book includes supporting research behind assets and their proven, positive impact on youth; celebration of programs' strengths; examples of engaging staff and leadership in introducing and using assets; and ideas for becoming more intentional with asset building.

What's Working? Tools for Evaluating Your Mentoring Program

Assess your mentoring program's goals and progress with this functional resource. Based on tools developed by Search Institute to evaluate the Schools Plus Mentoring Program (a partnership between Pillsbury and Big Brothers Big Sisters), *What's Working?* includes surveys, focus group questions, and interview protocols that allow you to gather information from mentors, mentees, parents, and teachers/other adults.

115

Working Shoulder to Shoulder: Stories and Strategies of Youth-Adult Partnerships That Succeed

Looking for a way to enhance your organization's involvement with youth? How about inviting youth to the table? *Working Shoulder to Shoulder* is filled with inspiring, true stories about youth and adult partnerships and practical steps to get positive relationships started. In their own words, adults and youth describe the barriers they've encountered, lessons they've learned, and successes they've shared. The book provides tips, ideas, and practical wisdom and advice from people engaged in real youth-adult partnerships. Here you'll find a step-by-step guide to starting and building partnerships.

RESOURCES FOR MENTORS

Tag, You're It! 50 Easy Ways to Connect with Young People

Get inspired and motivated with this asset-building idea book! Written in an easy-to-read format, *Tag, You're It!* offers 50 commonsense ways for adults to connect and build assets with young people. Each inspirational idea contains a reference to a supportive research study or expert opinion and includes action items to help you journey toward positive change.

Conversations on the Go: Clever Questions to Keep Teens and Grown-Ups Talking

Looking for a fun way to encourage family and other youth–adult conversations? *Conversations on the Go* is bound to get you talking. The book is filled with intriguing questions, guaranteed to stretch the imagination and bring out each other's personality and true self. This stimulating, go-anywhere book gives teens and adults a chance to find out what the other thinks about the big questions and the little ones.

Just When I Needed You: True Stories of Adults Who Made a Difference in the Lives of Young People

Just When I Needed You is an inspiring collection of stories from adults about who was there for them when they were growing up, and how they've made an impact on the young people they know today. Each story comes from the heart as the storyteller describes a critical moment or relationship that made the difference in her or his life. Both inspiring and instructive, this book shows just how much of a difference we can make in the lives of young people all around us.

150 Ways to Show Kids You Care /
Los Niños Importan: 150 Maneras de Demostrárselo

Even the simplest acts of kindness can build assets in the lives of children. This warm, inviting, and colorful book provides adults easy ideas and meaningful reminders about how they can show kids they really care. Based on the best-selling poster of the same name, *150 Ways to Show Kids You Care* is the perfect gift for parents, teachers, babysitters, youth workers, yourself, and anyone who touches the lives of kids, especially those ages 10 and younger. Includes an introduction to the Developmental Asset categories and 150 ideas in both English and Spanish.

"Ask Me Where I'm Going" and Other
Revealing Messages from Today's Teens

This intimate little book will touch your heart as you read poignant and practical "real words" from teens—describing what they really want from the caring adults in their lives. "Let me share my worries with you . . . Never give up on me . . . Encourage me more, criticize me less." A perfect gift book for anyone who touches the lives of teens. Based on the popular *In Our Own Words* posters.

Who, Me? Surprisingly Doable Ways You Can
Make a Difference for Kids (calendar)

"Today, I will do something to let the young people in my life know I care." Use this desktop perpetual calendar for reminders, tips, and inspiration in your daily interactions with children and teens. Here you'll find 366 great, concrete asset-building ideas.

You Can Make a Difference for Kids

This engaging eight-page booklet shows how anyone can and should build Developmental Assets. Developed in partnership with 3M, this booklet introduces the concept of asset building in a fun and accessible way and motivates its readers to take simple steps to build assets for young people in their families or communities. The booklet includes tear-out cards with the asset lists for each age group of children and teenagers from birth through age 18.

RESOURCES FOR MENTEES

Me @ My Best: Ideas for Staying True to Yourself—Every Day

This booklet was inspired by the voices of many young people throughout North America who know Developmental Assets and how to communicate the power of "keeping it real" to their peers. Speaking directly to young people, the booklet introduces the framework in a youth-friendly way, encourages them to explore what the categories mean to them personally, and inspires them to find and build upon their own strengths.

Take It to the Next Level: Making Your Life What You Want It to Be

Created just for teens and young adolescents, *Take It to the Next Level* helps young people focus on their successes, explore what they really want and how to get it, and celebrate their efforts and accomplishments. Filled with activities and journal topics, this booklet guides young people through the journey of adolescence from a Developmental Assets approach. A companion booklet to Search Institute's *Me @ My Best*, *Take It to the Next Level* offers young people a chance to take the assets deeper by offering opportunity for more self exploration and action.

Step by Step! A Young Person's Guide to Positive Community Change

This workbook gives young people the skills, ideas, and motivation they need to bring about positive change in their community. Written by youth and youth workers, it will help young people identify neighborhood and community issues, brainstorm possibilities for change, and recruit adults to work with them to develop and implement community change plans.

RESOURCES FOR FAMILIES OF MENTEES

Connect 5: Finding the Caring Adults You May Not Realize Your Teen Needs

Parents don't have to be all things at all times for their teens, and many teens yearn for more warm, trusting relationships with caring adults. In *Connect 5*, author (and mother) Kathleen Kimball-Baker provides hope, encouragement, and practical advice for parents and caregivers who wish to reach out and help their teens connect with other responsible and supportive adults, a critical factor in their healthy development.

Parenting at the Speed of Teens: Positive Tips on Everyday Issues

Parenting at the Speed of Teens is a practical, easy-to-use guide that offers positive, commonsense strategies for dealing with both the everyday issues of parenting teenagers—junk food, the Internet, stress, jobs, friends—and other serious issues teens may encounter—depression, divorce, racism, substance abuse. It illustrates how the daily "little things," such as talking one-on-one, setting boundaries, offering guidance, and modeling positive behavior, make a big difference in helping a teenager be successful during these challenging, exciting years of adolescence.

WHY Do They Act That Way? A Survival Guide to the Adolescent Brain for You and Your Teen

Even smart kids do stupid things. It's a simple fact of life. No one makes it through the teenage years unscathed—not the teens and not their parents. But now there's expert help for both generations in this groundbreaking new guide for surviving the drama of adolescence. In *WHY Do They Act That Way?*, National Institute on Media and Family's president and award-winning psychologist, Dr. David Walsh, explains exactly what happens to the human brain on the path from childhood into adolescence and adulthood. Revealing the latest scientific findings in easy-to-understand terms, Dr. Walsh shows why moodiness, quickness to anger and to take risks, miscommunication, fatigue, territoriality, and other familiar teenage behavior problems are so common—all are linked to physical changes and growth in the adolescent brain. (Published by Free Press, 2004)

Raising Kids Who Thrive pamphlet set

Originally developed by health care professionals who wanted something to hand out at wellness checkups, these pamphlets easily introduce parents and caregivers to the asset message and to information about ways to raise healthy, thriving kids. Engaging and encouraging, these pamphlets remind parents and caregivers of their central role in the physical, emotional, and social development of their children. What's more, they offer dozens of tips on everyday issues and ideas for how parents can give their kids the support, guidance, and connectedness they need to thrive.

Conversations on the Go: Clever Questions to Keep Teens and Grown-Ups Talking

Looking for a fun way to encourage family and other youth–adult conversations? *Conversations on the Go* is bound to get you talking. The book is filled with intriguing questions, guaranteed to stretch the imagination and bring out each other's personality and true self. This stimulating, go-anywhere book gives teens and adults in their family a chance to find out what the other thinks about the big questions and the little ones.

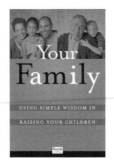

Your Family: Using Simple Wisdom in Raising Your Children

All families need as much confidence and support as they can get. This compact booklet helps parents and caregivers reflect on their important role—and the power they have—to bring good things into the lives of their children. By introducing the concept of Developmental Assets as simple wisdom supported by compelling research, the booklet is a perfect tool for strengthening the positive qualities of families. It concisely provides parents and caregivers with easy-to-follow summaries of the eight asset categories and what these areas of development mean to their children.

MVPARENTS.com Created by Search Institute, this is an online resource for busy, caring parents who want information they can trust about raising responsible children and teens. Here they'll find easy, time-tested ideas and tools to guide their kids in making smart choices and avoiding potential pitfalls. Parents can count on this Web site to cheer them on as they "stay in the game" and become the Most Valuable Parents they can be.